Paint and Patches

Painting on Fabric with Pigments

Paint and Patches

Painting on Fabric with Pigments

by VICKI L. JOHNSON

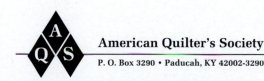

American Quilter's Society

P. O. Box 3290 • Paducah, KY 42002-3290

PLATE I-1 (RIGHT). *PUPPIES ON THE BEACH, 27" x 27", Vicki L. Johnson, Soquel, California, © 1991. Photo by George R. Young. Beach scenes need people or something in them to give them scale. Adding my puppies and husband on the beach makes the quilt more personal. You do not have to be detailed about the people, just a suggestion works.*

Library of Congress Cataloging-in-Publication Data

Johnson, Vicki L.
      Paint and patches : painting on fabric with pigments/ Vicki L.
Johnson.
           p.   cm.
      Includes bibliographical references and indexes.
      ISBN 0-89145 -856-5
      1. Textile painting.   2. Patchwork.   3. Machine appliqué.
   4. Machine quilting.   5. Quilts.   I. Title.
   TT851.J63   1995
   746.46--dc20   95--38143
                                                                    CIP

Additional copies of this book may be ordered from:

American Quilter's Society
P.O. Box 3290
Paducah, KY 42002-3290
@18.95. Add $2.00 for postage and handling.

Printed by **IMAGE GRAPHICS, INC.**, Paducah, Kentucky

DEDICATED TO

Terry Wilder Johnson, my husband, who has been there through all the agonies and joys helping me and pushing me. Without him I could not have continued taking the risks necessary to develop my art.

My mother, J. Louise Sears Larson, and my grandmothers, Georgia May Reeder Sears and Alice Lundeen Larson, the people who believed in me as an artist before anyone else. They are in my heart and with me in spirit while I work.

Ted Laurence Johnson, my son, who urged me to take that first desktop publishing class so I learned how to use the computer, which made this book possible to write. He patiently edited the first article I ever had published, which gave me the confidence to continue.

My father, R. L. Larson, who never accepted a thought that I would not go on to college and who provided that education for me. This all began with those courses.

CONTENTS

Plate I-2. *SEALS AND KELP, 6' x 8', Vicki L. Johnson, Soquel, California, © 1990. Collection of the Oregon Coast Aquarium, Newport, Oregon. Photo courtesy of the Oregon Coast Aquarium. This quilt was done in three panels so they would move in the breeze, just as kelp moves in the water. Doing a triptych is a challenge in design, because each panel should work alone and with the others. Having the paint colors and quilting lines flow between the three while working on this large a scale was also difficult.*

INTRODUCTION

Combining painting with patchwork was a very exciting idea to me. My background includes painting with watercolors, oils, and acrylics so it seemed a natural thing to do after I discovered quilts. Neither of my grandmothers quilted to my knowledge. My Nana, my maternal grandmother, was an excellent seamstress and lived with us. She never actually taught me sewing, but just being around her and sewing doll clothes with a bit of her help was an education.

To me, until I saw a quilt in an art and craft exhibit, quilts were just the bedcoverings one purchased at a store. I never had them in my background so the traditional work was just as new to me as the contemporary work. The designs and techniques of both have been exciting and I have used both in my work.

While living in Mendocino, quite isolated from all the stimulating classes and conferences happening in the quilt world, I developed my painted quilts. Using the charming town as my inspiration, I did many quilts while I was there. Now I still live along the coast of California, but on the Monterey Bay. The natural world around me is a source of ideas for my quilts. I find it is best to use what is most familiar and loved.

While looking through the quilts in this book, be sure to note the dates and remember they took many years to make. Each one builds on the previous and you can see how ideas progress from quilt to quilt. For me, making quilts is like taking a journey for which I do not know the destination, but find the trip very rewarding in itself.

This book was written with all the students I have had over the years in mind. There may be things in it you already know, but others do not. Some students have come to me with extensive painting and design knowledge. They only need to find how paints work on fabric and how the colors mix. Others have never even tried to paint before. Anyone who wants to can do a painting. I have tried to give you the instruction you need to get started. Play around with the paints, do the painting exercises, or plunge in and try to do a painting. Everyone has a different working pattern and any of these will do. The important thing is to have fun and not to tense up.

One of my students in a two-day class took home her leftover paint for her children. She had been very discouraged because she had never painted before and was very tense while trying. Once her children had the paints, they played around and had several paintings in a short time. She came back to class with a more playful, relaxed attitude and finished two charming paintings the second day.

Some of the things I have written about were discovered only after doing many quilts. Some I am working on still. Each time I do a painting I find something new to try. Your very first painting will not be your best, even if you are very pleased with it. Most artists do many to have one good one. Art conservationists are always discovering paintings under other paintings. An artist working in oils just painted over the one she did not like and tried again. Watercolorists often wash off the unwanted work and start over with a toned paper. Quilters can cut up paintings and use the fabric for piecing. Remembering this may help you loosen up and relax with your work.

I suggest reading through Chapter 1 to familiarize yourself with the general information about the paint. Then you can use the paint exercises to learn more specifics. Go through the exercises and do them as you go. If you have painted before, they should acquaint you quickly with the differences in this paint from other traditional media and you will be ready to do your own work. Those who have not painted before should continue working with the book as a guide through Chapter 4.

Throughout the book, making a small wall quilt 24" x 30" is used as a sample project to guide you in the techniques presented. You, of course, can elect to do any size quilt or to just play with the new methods.

After the painting, I do soft-edge appliqué. It is a simple concept, but there are ways to make it easier and they are explained in Chapter 5. Other quilters who do a similar technique seem to have their own approach to it. Mine gives you a sturdy,

washable piece that has a finished look.

You can continue with the format of a 24" x 30" wall quilt in Chapter 6, which is about the border treatment used. To finish the quilt, it is machine quilted, but with the approach of a stitcher. Once completed, the next step is to display and exhibit the new creation and methods for this are discussed in Chapter 10. The book concludes with thoughts and methods for expanding into larger quilts.

A very serious attitude can be important in giving you the drive to continue with your art, but most artists are also children at heart. Have fun, but keep at it. I hope this book helps to guide your play.

PLATE 1-3. *PIGEON PT. BARNS, 27" x 30", Vicki L. Johnson, Soquel, California, © 1991. Photo by Charley Lynch. These barns sit near the Pigeon Pt. lighthouse, which I have used in several quilts. They are too far away to be placed close to the lighthouse, but I liked them enough to do a quilt with just the barns.*

PLATE I-4. *SARA'S GALLERY, 42" x 42", Vicki L. Johnson, Mendocino, California, © 1984. Private collection. After doing several large quilts with most of the buildings along Main Street in Mendocino, I was ready for something different. This building sits at the west end of town and was the site of the Long Britton gallery. My friend, Sara Long, was a co-owner and is a quiltmaker. Many of the touches in this quilt reflect things about her. The squares in the border repeat a favorite origami paper fold she used in her paper pieces. Her quilts have a Japanese feeling to them, accomplished with fabrics found mostly at garage sales. I resorted to using actual Japanese fabric for the larger squares to capture this feeling. The VW parked on the road was hers, too. Adding personal touches makes the quilt more interesting and fun to do. I was particularly pleased with the contrast between the dark Cypress trees and the buildings on this quilt.*

SECTION I

AN INTRODUCTION
TO
PAINTS AND PAINTING

Chapter 1

Information about the Paint

Painting on fabric is a new and exciting technique to us, but it has been done in the past. I have a set of paints given to me by a friend, which we think are from the 1920's, but they could be older. Crazy quilts often have painted motifs on the fabric shapes instead of embroidery. In the Shelburne Museum, there is a quilt dated c. 1850 which has black spatter painting on it in the squares between pieced blocks. In some books I have seen painted scenes with embroidery worked on them from the early 1800's. The Plains Indians did elaborate paintings on leather, which often told stories. I am not sure what paints these other makers used, but those available in the past were quite different from today's paints. India ink, oil paints, and watercolors were probably used.

Today we have new materials. We have easy-to-use permanent paints that are mixed with water. These are the same paints commercial printers are using to silkscreen fabrics. Most of the fabrics we buy today are silkscreened, so the fabric you paint is as colorfast and washable as the fabric you buy. These new paints are nontoxic and easily set with an iron, which makes them simple and safe.

Since they were formulated for use in silkscreening, the paints naturally smooth out. This is an advantage if you want a solid, smooth area.

For my work, I wanted to duplicate some of the painterly textures I was used to in working with oils or watercolors. What I discovered was how to achieve special effects and keep the paint from running on the fabric when I did not want it to. The textures I achieved did not duplicate oil or watercolor effects, but were exciting in themselves. This is what I would like to share with you in this section of the book.

Dye reacts with the fiber of the fabric and makes a chemical bond with it, becoming a part of the fiber. Paint contains pigment that bonds with the fabric, but sits on the fiber rather than becoming part of it. For my work I use paint rather than dye because I find it easier to use and control.

The particular brands of paint I use are Versatex™ and Createx™. There are many others on the market, but these are easy to find. They leave the fabric soft to the hand.

SAFE USES

When I was first experimenting with different techniques and materials, I studied dyes. Most were very toxic and required extremely careful use. All required steam setting, a complicated procedure. I am concerned for my health and do have allergies, so the toxicity worried me. Dyes are now available which do not need steaming, but they are still more complicated to use than the paint.

The paints I use are labeled nontoxic, but I am still careful and you should be, too. Do not eat and paint at the same time. Use containers different from those you use for cooking. If you are doing a very messy technique that requires immersing your hands in the paint for long periods, use rubber gloves. Lightweight ones are available from the same sources as the paints. The paints are supposed to be safe, but a little care in their use can protect you from unknown problems.

ABOUT THE PAINT

Versatex™ comes in three starter sets of eight two-ounce jars. Set 1 provides you the colors the manufacturer considers basic, including white and black. That really is all you need for colors, but I always want to have everything available. To get all the colors I regularly use, I have to buy all three starter sets. It will be more economical for you to buy the starter sets, rather than individual jars of my 10 basic colors. (These colors are listed under materials needed for the exercises.) A two-ounce jar is enough paint for several small quilts. It should last a long time unless you do a very large project, like a queen-size quilt. Then you may want to buy four-ounce jars of the colors for that quilt. You will also need the extender and a four-ounce jar is a good size with which to begin.

Versatex™ comes in pearlescent, fluorescent, and metallic colors and an opaque white. However, I use Createx™ because I find their pearlescents and metallics have more shimmer and their covering white is extremely opaque. I have had no problems using Createx™ and Versatex™ together. Unless your local art supply store carries Createx™, you will have to place a minimum order of $25.00 at this writing, from Color Craft. It is easy to run up that amount as they have many wonderful colors, but ordering all Versatex™ may be easier when just starting. Createx™ has a product called Bond-All, which helps the paint adhere better. I have found a few drops of Bond-All, in the Createx™ pearlescent paint is necessary when it is used thickly.

Versatex™ has airbrush ink for use in an airbrush, but it is the same paint. The pigments have been ground finer and more are added. It is diluted to a consistency good for hand painting. Since the color is more intense, some artists prefer the airbrush ink to the regular paint, but it is more expensive. Rubber stamps work particularly well with the ink, since the color is more intense.

The paint stores well for a long time, some colors better than others. I have had jars that lasted years. When the paint begins to coagulate and seem sticky, it is beginning to go bad. You can continue to use it, but it becomes hard to spread, so I usually replace a deteriorating jar. Once I had a jar of royal blue that smelled strongly like gasoline, so I called the company and they said not to use it. I did try it and it worked, but the fabric retained the smell. This odor was very strong, not the usual smell of the paint. Otherwise, the paint is good until it becomes dried out. Once hard, it cannot be softened. If you find mold on the paint, just scrape it off. It will still work fine; I do this all the time. To protect the paint in the jar, you could try using only

PLATE 1-1.
This set of paints was given to me by Henry Dewenter after his great-aunt died. As best we know they were from the 1920's, but there are no dates on them or the literature with them. Paints of this type could have been used on fabric for quilts.

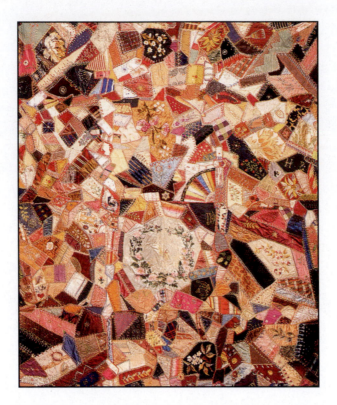

PLATE 1-2. *SELTENREICH CRAZY QUILT, 56" x 56", Unknown maker c. 1890. Private collection. Photo by Mert Carpenter. On this crazy quilt from the Seltenreich family are many hand-painted fabrics.*

PLATES 1-3, 1-4, AND 1-5. *SELTENREICH CRAZY QUILT. Details of Plate 1-2. Photos by Mert Carpenter.*
LEFT: *The initials are painted by hand and the S is backwards. In Quilter's Newsletter June 1994, quilt historian Merikay Waldvogel suggests a quilter may have made her S backward because she was illiterate. This may also explain the backward S painted on this quilt.*
CENTER: *Some of the flowers are quite sophisticated in design and may be painted on top of a printed fabric, since the design continues beyond the shape used. They may also have been painted by a different person.*
RIGHT: *Since the maker or makers are gone, the family does not know who actually made this quilt. It has several initials on it, so perhaps it was a friendship quilt. This painted wreath has a K in the center.*

distilled water when mixing water into the jar itself. Usually, I mix paint in a different jar and do not return paint to the original jar; I keep old spice bottles to save leftovers.

There is a source list at the end of this book listing mail-order suppliers for all the materials I use.

FABRIC

The paints work on any natural fiber, which includes cotton, linen, silk, viscose rayon, and leather. If you want to use a blend or a manmade fabric, Versatex™ has a binder that can be added in small amounts to help the paint adhere. Createx™ Bond-All will help with their paints. It is especially good to use a few drops with the pearlescent paint, even when painting on cotton.

For most of my work I use a white cotton lawn that I purchase from Testfabrics™. It is a lightweight fabric, but of very good quality. When purchasing fabric from a store, ask if there is any finish applied to it. If it wrinkles when scrunched in your fist, there is probably no finish. Prewash the fabric in regular laundry detergent. That should remove any sizing.

When I was doing dye work, I purchased fabric from the store, washed it, and then dyed it. Often the fabric would not take the dye. It was not the store's fault; they had sold me 100% cotton. There was some treatment or finish that did not wash out, one of which the store was unaware. It always seemed as though once I did find a fabric brand that worked well, the store would discontinue it. These problems led me to Testfabrics™. They make fabric that is ready to dye. No finishes or treatment that prevent the dye from taking are used on it. I use their fabric to paint on, so finish is not such a potential problem. The paint takes to most fabrics, but my dyeing experience has made me wary. For the samples in Chapter 3, I did use solid-colored fabric from the store and had no problems with Versatex™ on these fabrics.

Although fabric from Testfabrics™ is supposedly ready to dye with no prewashing, I wash it.

Some of it shrinks quite a bit, so I wash primarily to preshrink. The amount of shrinkage for quilts is not so much of a problem, but in clothing it is. Since I prewash all my fabrics, I prewash the fabric from Testfabrics™, that way there is no potential for shrinkage.

Ironing the fabric before painting is not necessary as it smoothes out once it is wet. I do iron before drawing to make it easier for tracing onto the fabric. The smooth fabric is easier to see through.

Many of the fabrics from Testfabrics™ are quite wide, which is an advantage I like. The cotton lawn I use is 54" wide, so I can make a large quilt with no seams in the painting. They have even wider fabric available and many other selections.

Using a lightweight fabric helps to retain a soft hand. The paint pigment adds stiffness to the fabric. More paint means stiffer fabric. Heavyweight fabric with very thick paint becomes like plastic. The combination of Versatex™ and cotton lawn allows me to use enough paint for color intensity and yet retain a soft hand.

BRUSHES AND OTHER MATERIALS

For most of my painting, I use No. 6 round (about as round as my little finger) and No. 8 flat (about 1" wide) brushes. Since I am a former oil paint, watercolor, and acrylic painter, having a supply of brushes of different sizes is no problem, but I find these two the most useful. However, using brushes you also use with oil paint is not a good idea, since the water softens the bristles. If there should be any oil paint residue from previous painting, the chemical mixes may not stand up over time even if the color looks good at first. Any watercolor or acrylic painting brushes will work with the fabric paint. Eventually, you will collect a wide variety for different purposes.

The brushes wear out much faster than when used on paper, so expensive ones are not a good investment. The rougher fabric surface seems to wear them down quickly. I spend about $10.00 to $15.00 dollars for a brush. That usually purchases one of good enough quality to last and to hold a point. If they are too cheap the bristles fall out while you work, which is very annoying. Other shapes can be useful to have. A fan, scriptliner, very fine, very wide, or stiff ones like stenciling brushes are all good ones to have if you plan to do more painting.

Take good care of your brushes and they will last longer. Clean them as soon as you finish working. Versatex™ does not seem to harden irreversibly in the brush, but I try not to leave them unwashed for long. While working on this book, I accidentally left a wide brush full of pearlescent paint out over night. It seemed impossible to remove, but I persisted by soaking it in water and then gently rubbing the paint out. After several soakings I had the brush usable. Do not wash brushes in water hot to the touch as it loosens the glue holding the bristles. Resting brushes on their bristles will eventually leave them bent. Rinse them a bit in water while you work and lay them on the table, rather than

PLATE 1-6.
Most of my painting is done with the first two brushes on the left. The next tool is a palette knife, used to mix paint. From left to right the other brushes are: a fine brush for fine lines; a scriptliner used to make fine, long lines such as tree branches; a fan brush good for making palm trees, pine trees, or blending; a fat brush for bushes; another fat one with long bristles, which holds a lot of paint when you want to cover a large area; a three-inch cheap house painter's brush which is great for covering large areas with extender or washes.

leaving them in the water jar. This will also keep the wood from swelling and loosening the ferrule.

Another item you will need to find at an art supply store is an elephant ear sponge. These are fine-grain small natural sponges often sold in the ceramics department. They are sometimes called flat seasilk sponges. Another good sponge is a sea-wool. You can find these sponges at chain drugstores sold as makeup sponges and bath sponges for half the price. Natural sponges give a better texture than manmade for the landscapes. Any sponge will work with the paint and I encourage you to try any you can find, even the manmade ones.

You will also need a container to hold water. Since plastic does not break, it is safest. A palette can be anything that holds the paint for you. A microwave plate with a cover works well because the cover allows you to save the paint for a few days. But, you can also cover a palette with plastic wrap or a bowl. Have an old piece of fabric or some paper towels available for wiping brushes and palette knives.

Art supply stores have palette knives in many types and sizes. One as pictured (PLATE 1-6) for mixing paint is very useful, but you can substitute a table knife. Take the paint out of the jar with a palette knife and mix with it on the palette. This keeps brushes and the paint in the jar clean. Some oil painters like to paint with these knives, so there are varying shapes available. I encourage you to experiment with anything you fancy. Usually, I do not paint with a palette knife, because it lays the paint on too thick, which stiffens the fabric.

You now have enough basics to start.

HEAT-SETTING

After all the work of painting, it is important to heat-set the paint very, very well. This is not difficult, but should be done with care. It is especially important to heat-set thicker paint for a longer time. Set the paints with an iron. At the correct setting for the fabric used, iron the piece at least four times. I put the ironing board where I can be comfortable for awhile and I open a window. It does give off a smell, but is supposed to be nontoxic. Then I very slowly iron each side in two directions, turning the piece to change direction and turning it over to do the back (Figure 1-1). That way I have covered every area with no areas left out.

For most of my quilts I used my iron without a press sheet and found it to work well. Until I started to use colored pearlescent paints, the paint never transferred to the iron, but sometimes the pearlescents do. Now I have found a nonstick press sheet, which is supposed to increase the adherence of the paint to the fabric. I painted a pair of pants using a lot of spattered pearlescent paint, and when I washed them much of the paint came out. The iron did not slide easily over the thick, uneven paint so I missed many areas. With the press sheet, this is not a problem. The manufacturer claims using it when the paint is fresh helps to make it adhere. When I used it on almost dry paint, the wet areas transferred to the press sheet. Ironing them with the sheet still in place until they were dry did make the paint adhere to the fabric. However, I think using it immediately after the paint is dry is the best. That way there is no chance of smearing. The press sheet directs the heat to the fabric, but helps to prevent scorching. So far I am pleased with the results. The sheets are like plastic and become very hot; therefore, care is needed to let it cool a moment before touching so you do not burn yourself. The press sheet is also useful when using iron-on interfacing, since the glue will rub off.

When using a heavily napped fabric like cotton velour, the paint can be set in the dryer. After the paint is dry, put it in the dryer for 40 minutes at the highest heat. When I did this, I found much of the color became lighter than it was originally. It may be that much of the paint was caught between the fibers rather than actually attached to them. It is always a good idea to test before doing any major work. The effect was still nice and usable, just much softer than planned.

The paint can be used on any natural fiber,

PLATE 1-7.
This is how I have my painting area set up when working on small quilts. Just about anything works to hold the paint, but I like a piece of glass taped to a white cardboard backing. Many artists use a white butcher's metal tray available at most art suppliers. The important thing is to mix paint on a white background because anything colored or dark will affect the way you see the colors. My table is white and the paints clean up readily, so I use it to back the fabric. Again, it is important to have a white background because the fabric becomes translucent when wet. You could also cover a piece of cardboard as large as the fabric with white plastic.

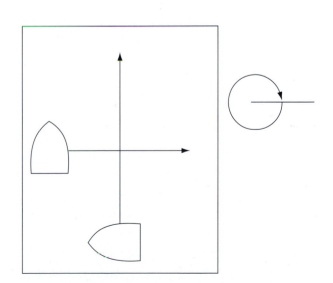

FIGURE 1-1.
Four directions to iron. Turn over and repeat.

including leather. I have painted on chamois, which worked like painting on paper. To heat-set, let it dry completely and then put it in a dryer for 40 minutes at the hottest temperature. Again, testing would be a good idea, especially if you plan to wash the item repeatedly later.

WASHING

Once the painting has been well set, it can be washed in the washing machine. For my landscapes, I do the soft-edge appliqué before washing, but after heat-setting. When I first started, I washed the painting in the same soap I was using to do the laundry. At that time, it was a pure soap. Now I wash all my fabrics and the paintings in Orvus®. I have become more aware of the concerns of textile conservationists and believe this gives my quilts the best chance of survival. Orvus® rinses out completely and does not leave a harmful soap residue. I even wash my clothes in it now, because I have developed an allergy to soap. Many laundry detergents have bleach in their formula. Knowing which ones do is difficult, so you are taking a chance with your quilt if you use them. This can be hard on your quilt and you may not know until the damage is done. Since Orvus® is recommended by textile conservationists for washing quilts, why not start using it from the beginning?

A small jar of Orvus® can be purchased because it just takes one tablespoon for a small painting. In an article from a textile conservationist on washing quilts, she said they used five tablespoons of Orvus® to wash a quilt. From that as a guide, I have been using just one tablespoon for a medium-size load of clothes. This should give you an idea of the amount for your project. If you find you are using it frequently, Orvus® can be purchased at feed stores in very large containers cheaper than in the small size. It is horse or sheep soap, depending on the animals in your area.

Once you have gathered your materials, I would suggest you do the following exercises with the paint. Even if you are an experienced painter, these paints react a little differently from any of the traditional media. You especially need to become aware of the use of the extender. It is the secret to controlling the paint on fabric.

MATERIALS:

FABRIC

Minimum of one yard any 100% pre-washed cotton fabric.

PALETTE

Something to hold the paint. Clean TV dinner trays work fine – the kind with a microwave cover is especially good, since the cover prevents the paint drying out if stored overnight.

BRUSHES

WATER CONTAINER

Anything that holds water – plastic preferred for safety.

PLASTIC-COVERED CARDBOARD

You can paint on a large piece of cardboard covered with white plastic bags. White is important because a dark-colored bag will create a dark area when the fabric is wet. This will make you think the colors are darker than they really are. The directions will be for a piece approximately 13" x 16", so your cardboard should be approximately 18" x 18". If you want to work larger, adjust the size to at least 1" larger than the fabric.

PLASTIC

To cover your working surface so cleanup is easier. If you prefer, you can paint on a plastic-covered work surface and forget the cardboard.

PENCIL

Soft No. 2, to write on fabric.

PAPER TOWELS OR RAG

PALETTE KNIFE

ELEPHANT EAR OR OTHER NATURAL SPONGES

SMALL PAPER CUPS

At least two containers are needed for mixing while doing the fabric painting exercises.

RULER, SCISSORS, OLD TOOTHBRUSH

PAINT

If you have the three starter sets and a jar of extender, you have all the paint colors needed to do these exercises. Otherwise, you will need the following colors:

Extender	White
Sky Blue	Red
Orange	Green
Royal Blue	Ocher
Blue	Violet
Brown	Pearlescent (optional)

Wear old clothes!

PLATE 1-8, (BELOW). *DAY/NITE, 58" x 50", Vicki L. Johnson, Mendocino, California, © 1981. Private collection. To create this quilt I had to do two complete paintings and then cut them up. It seemed like a simple idea, but proved to be quite difficult because of the need for seam allowances. Doing the two paintings so they matched was easy. I made a master line drawing, which I traced onto the fabric by using my window as a light box. To make the guides for cutting the pieces, I had to put the paintings on my drafting table and draw each square with its seam allowance and the angle at the corner. In the summer of 1981, a very creative time, I did four quilts shown in Plates 1-8, 1-9, 1-10, and 8-1 (detail). Each of these four was the beginning of a series which I continue to work on.*

PLATE 1-9. *MENDOCINO, 32" x 38", Vicki L. Johnson, Mendocino, California,*
© *1981. Private collection. The original concept for this quilt was to have very abstract*
shapes representing the buildings scattered at the top above the meadow. As I worked
they became more realistic, but the meadow did remain loose. In it are machine embroi-
dered lines done in the same direction as the quilting. Both used thicker applications of
thread. The border uses 1½" squares to repeat the shape of the buildings, graduating
from blues in the sky to browns and earth colors below. This was the first in my series of
Mendocino quilts.

PLATE 1-10. *THE HAUN BARN, 58" x 49", Vicki L. Johnson, Mendocino, California, © 1981. Private collection. Photo by George R. Young. Painting this scene was a challenge because I wanted to use a special time of day on the California coast, just as the sun is setting, which gives everything a pink glow. It took four layers of paint and several on-site trips to look at the color to capture that pink. This time I wanted the squares to flow in and out of the meadow and hand appliquéd them on top. I have used this same barn in several more recent quilts.*

Chapter 2

Painting Exercises

Before beginning a landscape or other painting, I suggest you try these exercises. Once you have done them, you will have covered basic instruction in controlling the paint, techniques, and color mixing. Even if you are familiar with painting, these paints handle and mix a bit differently from the more traditional media.

PREPARATION

Gather the supplies in the list at the end of Chapter 1. Set up a painting area where you do not have to disturb your work for several days. The paints wash off hard surfaces such as Formica readily, but I usually protect my tabletop with plastic so I do not have to clean it. You can see the setup I use in PLATE 1-7 page 19. Figure 2-1 is a chart you will be following to do these exercises. It may be helpful if you photocopy it so you can have it beside you while you work. You do not have to do all the sections of the chart at one sitting. To do it all will probably take three hours. Working quickly is best. A good breaking point for a second session is just before the color mixing. Spending time with the colors is more beneficial than the other sections, so adjust your time to have half of it for the mixing.

Fill your water container and put small (½ teaspoon) dots of paint onto your palette. Be sure to place extender and white paint on your palette. Note where you put the extender. It is easy to confuse it with the white paint. Extender looks more translucent, rather like yogurt, and white paint is more like cottage cheese. If you get them confused, try mixing what you think is white with a very little red. If it does not go quite pink, you probably have the extender. Or smear, with your finger, the white and extender onto a dark surface. The extender will be much more transparent than the white.

Tear or cut a piece of fabric approximately 15" x 15". If you know you like to splash paint around freely, cut a bigger piece. Also, cut a piece about 3" x 5". This small piece will be used for section 5 of your chart.

You will need to create lines on your fabric corresponding to the lines on the chart. The easiest way is to fold the fabric in fourths lengthwise and finger press. Then fold it in fourths the other direction. This should make a grid of four sections across and four down. Usually the fold lines are enough of a guide. To make them more obvious you may want to draw these lines with a pencil or felt-tip pen. Some people find it helpful to number the spaces to correspond to the chart. Be sure to follow the same numbering as the chart. There are more numbers than spaces.

It is not necessary to tape the fabric to your plastic, but some people find it helpful. Once the fabric is wet it will stick to the plastic. The plastic must be secured to the table or around a piece of cardboard so it does not move.

Place the chart where you can see it while working, or write the captions on your fabric. A photocopy is useful so you do not have to refer back to the chart in the book while following the directions. You may want to label the fabric chart, but it is not necessary. Do not be alarmed if you paint in the wrong section. This always happens in my classes and we just relabel the paper chart or fabric. This exercise is only to try the paints. You do not even have to follow the chart if your working style is really free and loose. You may never look at it again, or you may find the color section is useful later as a guide for mixing colors. I have even known students to cut their charts in pieces and use them in quilts. It makes very interesting fabric.

BASECOATS

Mix extender (about 25%) and water (about 75%) together in one of your small paper cups and paint it onto the small (3" x 5") piece of fabric. Set this aside until it dries for use later. Save the extender and water mixture for later use also. (The fabric piece will be for section 5.)

Paint on Fabric

In the first section of the chart, using sky blue paint as it comes from the jar, begin to paint from one of the corners and cover about ¼ of the section. The paint should feel thick and stiff. It is hard to spread unless you use lots of paint.

Put some of it on an area of your palette with the palette knife and mix in a little water. A mixture of about 25% water and 75% paint will work. Then try to paint with this mixture on another quarter of the section. It should spread better, but still is rather thick. Keep adding water to the paint and trying to paint with it. If you dilute it so much it runs everywhere, you will know what happens with too

much water. The paint works best mixed to the consistency of a thick sauce.

At different times you will want to vary the thickness of the paint. I try to use it thick enough to cover as intensely as I want, but as thin as I can so the hand of the fabric remains as soft as possible. If you put too much paint on, it makes the fabric feel like plastic. It is always a balancing act between enough paint for the effect wanted and as little paint as possible to keep the fabric soft.

Very Wet Paint on Wet Fabric

Using a clean brush, cover the second section with lots of water. Mix about 25% sky blue paint with 75% water in one of the paper cups. There should be enough color that you can see it when you use it. Paint with this mixture onto the area you covered with water.

The paint will want to run everywhere. As it dries, it will pool into interesting shapes with an edge of color. I like to use this very, very wet paint for areas like the sky. I paint in layers and often use very dilute paint for the first painting. You can enhance the pooling effect by painting in dots or short strokes without connecting them. As it dries the dots will bleed and may, or almost may, connect. This gives a more textured sky. Add a little more paint to the mixture and put it on with a large brush, and you can have a smooth wash of color.

People who paint with watercolors will be very comfortable with this technique. I find they want to use the very dilute color for everything. They are the only ones in class that I have to tell to use more paint. Most people are just the opposite. So if you are a watercolorist, keep this in mind. The fabric will want more paint or everything will run together. People who are oil painters have a difficult time adding enough water. Everyone else in fact, usually needs to add more water.

Very Wet Paint on Extender and Water

Cover section 3 with the same extender and water mixture you saved when you painted the

Fabric Painting Exercises Chart

Base Coats

1 paint on fabric	2 very wet paint on wet fabric	3 very wet paint on extender plus water	4 very wet paint with extender added on fabric	5 very wet paint on dried extender plus water

Techniques

6 stippling	7 spattering	8 sponging	9 scumbling

Color Mixing

10 glazing	11 & 12 pearlescent resist with wet in wet	13 royal blue & orange	14 sky blue & orange

Color Mixing

15 blue & orange	16 red & green	17 ochre & violet	18 green & –

FIGURE 2-1. *Fabric Painting Exercises Chart.*
Copy this chart on a copy machine and place it where you can see it while painting.

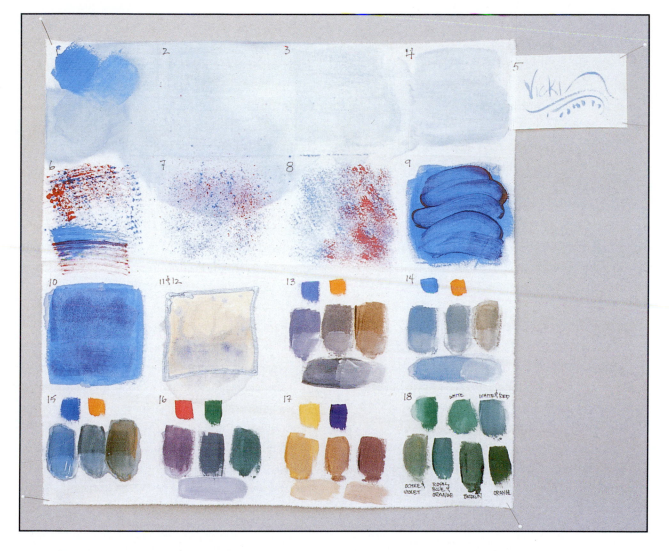

PLATE 2-1.
Use this completed chart as a guide while doing your own.

3" x 5" piece of fabric. Then paint onto this with the diluted paint mixture from section 2.

With the extender and water mixture as a basecoat, you should find the paint does not run as much and you have more control.

VERY WET PAINT WITH EXTENDER ADDED ON FABRIC

Mix the two mixtures from section 3 together in one of the cups. This will give you extender, water, and paint in a very wet mixture. Paint section 4 with this blend.

Adding extender to the paint is another way to control it. Depending on how much paint and extender you have, the paint will stay where you brushed it. Extender does not affect the hue of the color, it only thins it. This is quite useful, for instance, when you want a blush of red, but not pink. Adding white would give a very different look than thinning with extender.

VERY WET PAINT ON DRIED EXTENDER AND WATER

If your 3" x 5" piece of fabric has dried, try painting on it with the diluted paint and water mixture. Try using a small fine or well-pointed brush so you have thin lines. Writing your name will give you a test of this basecoat.

You should find painting on the dried extender is like painting on paper. It should give you much more control. You can first cover the fabric with the extender if you want the most control. It affects two different things. Adding extender as a layer does add pigment, so it adds to the stiffness of the fabric. The layer of extender gives a different textural look to the paint. As you gain experience, you will start to observe this difference and be able to choose which basecoat, if any, you want.

Once there is paint on the fabric it begins to act like a colored basecoat and many of the effects of using extender can be gained. This is the benefit of painting in several layers. By the time you are ready to add finishing detail, there is enough paint on the surface for you to have control.

TECHNIQUES

STIPPLING

With the old toothbrush, dip into some paint which has been thinned with a bit of water. The consistency of a thick sauce is a good place to start. Dab onto section 6 with the brush. An interesting texture should start to develop. Try using thicker and thinner paint to see what difference it makes.

Other types of brushes can be used to get different textures. Nail brushes, stenciling brushes, or just stiff paint brushes can be used. The texture is affected by the type of brush and the surface you stipple onto. A surface wet with water or paint will change the texture.

SPATTERING

For this you will want to cover anything within arm's length with something like paper towels or plastic as paint goes everywhere. Again with the toothbrush, dip into some paint which has been thinned with a bit of water. Holding the brush aimed at section 7, run your thumb over the bristles from the front to the back, so it creates a spatter.

The wetter the paint the larger the spatters. Try it with different dilutions. The layer you spatter onto will affect the texture. I use this for my underwater quilts, but my thumb becomes quite tired on a large piece. Another way to do this would be to run the brush on a piece of screen. Sometimes you can flip the brush, to create a line of spattered paint, which is also a nice effect.

SPONGING

Using your elephant ear sponge, cover section 8 with texture. A gentle dabbing or tapping motion works best. If you press too hard, you will just have blobs with no texture. Try this on wet fabric and on wet paint. Again the surface underneath will affect the texture.

For rocky cliffs or leafy foliage, natural sponges give great effects. Many beginners are more comfortable with a sponge than a brush. The only dan-

PLATE 2-2.

A stiff toothbrush is a great tool for spattering paint. This photo shows the position of the thumb and the brush to the fabric. Pull the thumb from the front to the back of the brush, flipping the bristles toward the fabric.

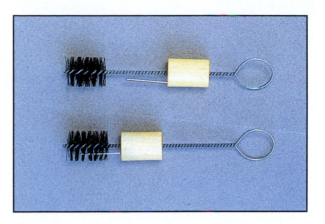

PLATE 2-3.

If your thumb is awkward or gets tired, you may want to try this spatterbrush. The nail is held against the bristles while you turn the brush. It gives a very fine spatter that really goes everywhere, so cover everything around you.

PLATE 2-4. *OUTER PLANETS, 25" x 25", Vicki L. Johnson, Soquel, California, © 1994. Photo: Charley Lynch. For this quilt, I painted on four Diamond Star blocks by spattering to create a look of galaxies. The paints work even on printed fabrics. Since I wanted the effect to be shiny, I used Createx™ pearlescent paint, which is quite opaque, so it worked well even on the dark fabric.*

ger is in overuse. Everything textured with the same sponge becomes boring.

SCUMBLING

Scumbling is a painting technique used with thick paint and a stiff brush. The brush is stroked in circular motions and enough pressure is applied to intermix the basecoat and the paint on the brush. Van Gogh would have used this technique.

Cover section 9 with sky blue paint used thick and wet. Then use your stiffest brush and thick, wet red paint to scumble into the blue. These two colors will mix and give interesting brush strokes. Resist the temptation to scrub the color in until it is smoothly blended. That can be done, but I want you to see how lovely the texture of the brush strokes are.

GLAZING

Glazing is done with a soft brush and very wet paint over dry paint. It can be done over wet paint

PLATE 2-5.
These are four examples of resists with the fabric paints. The whitest jelly fish is done with pearlescent paint – the others are various silk-painting resists. The gold silk-painting resist, like the paint, does not wash out. Both of the others wash out, so they work well as resists. The left one is very faint because I painted over it several times.

with a light touch of the soft brush. In the Renaissance, this was the technique used. Painters would do a painting of the forms completely in gray or brown tones. Then they would glaze the color on top. This saved on the very precious colored pigments. We are going to use this to change the color or value of an area which is already painted.

Usually, glazing is done over dry paint, but it is not necessary to let the paint dry for you to experience the technique. Cover section 10 with sky blue paint so it is quite blue. Then mix red paint with a lot of water, about as runny as cream. Use this to cover half of section 10, letting your brush strokes show. It can be done so the paint applied is very smooth, but I want you to see the possibilities of leaving brush strokes. The runny paint will want to smooth out.

Now add extender to the runny red paint. Use enough to make it thick and controllable, like thickening a sauce. Try this on the other half of section 10. With the extender added, you should regain control and be able to leave more brush strokes showing as it will not run and smooth out.

RESISTS

Resists are materials that prevent the paint from adhering to the fabric. An example is the use of wax in batik. You can use wax with these paints and other traditional resist techniques for use with waterbase media. Wax is difficult to remove and requires a very disciplined, orderly working method, so I do not use it.

I have only found two resist methods that are useful, but each has disadvantages. With our painter's approach, there is an added problem with resists that wash out. We are putting the paint on wet, usually with a brush or other tool that might smear the resist if it softens with water.

For painting on silk, there are resists available that wash out in water. These apply easily with brushes or other tools. Even after drying, they soften with the water in the paint, so a halo forms.

If you have acquired some of this, try it on one

of your sections. Put some on in a design or doodle, let it dry, and then paint over it.

The pearlescent paints can be used in a way that they become a resist. They do not wash out, so their color is a part of the work. I paint things like the foam of waves with white pearlescent before painting the blue ocean and let it dry. Then the waves remain white. If I do not do this, the blue may bleed into the wave.

To try this, outline section 11 with the pearlescent paint. If you have Createx™ paint in a squirt bottle top, use it to draw the line. The resist effect will be strongest if you let the paint dry first, but you can try it wet if you want to continue during the same working session. Paint very wet paint in the center of the section, as described in section 12, so wet it would bleed if it were not stopped by the pearlescent paint. The darker pearlescents will bleed if not dried, but this gives an interesting effect.

Another possibility for a resist is white glue. When I tried it, the effect was poor. The glue washes out since it is water soluble. It softened when the paint was applied. There was some effect of resist, but very misty looking. The silk painter's resist worked better.

Watercolorists sprinkle salt on the painted piece for interesting effects. Table salt does little to the fabric paint, but larger rock salt works. It leaves dots of white fabric showing wherever it lays. This is a type of resist and could be used for textural effects.

Wet in Wet

Painting with paint into wet paint with lots of water is a watercolorist's technique. It can be done successfully with these paints. To try it, add a different color into the wet paint in section 11. You can doodle anything – like a flower or just a design. Often this technique is used to add color into an area such as the blue shadows of a tree.

COLOR MIXING

Before you become comfortable with mixing colors, you will need to mix many. Once you

Plate 2-6. *PIGEON PT. BARNS, Vicki L. Johnson. Detail of Plate I-3, page 11. To make the waves white, I often paint them first with white pearlescent. When you use the very wet blue paint next to it, the dried pearlescent does not allow the blue to bleed into the wave area. You must be careful not to paint over the pearlescent or you will color it blue.*

Plate 2-7.
This technique of watercolorists is called wet in wet. The green tree was painted with wet paint and then the blue of the shadowed side was painted into the still-wet green. With fabric paints, it dries lighter, so another layer of color could be used for darker areas.

experience making a beautiful teal with orange and blue, then you will not have to think about it before mixing. When the basic mixes become automatic, then you will begin to do things freely. Reaching for the red to tone down a green will seem natural. With your color sense you have to feel it, and this takes a lot of experience. You may analyze later, but when it feels right that is when it is right.

Making a chart with many different possible mixes can help. I have several that I have done. I used to wonder what was wrong with me that I did not remember all the combinations I had used. Then I read that Georgia O'Keeffe had charts of her colors which she referred to when planning or working on a painting. That made me comfortable with my charts.

I have only one color rule. All colors go together. There are some that harmonize better, but all can be put together. Just observe nature – magenta flowers with orange ones, red and pink together, and blue with green everywhere. These combinations break three basic rules I grew up hearing. If you put rules like these in front of your eyes, you will use color by rote and not what you see or feel. Quilters seem to be prone to color rules. One of the first I heard was that warm reds should not be used with cool reds. Since I had worked with color in

painting, I just ignored the advice of the quilt shop salesperson and made my rail fence with a spectrum of reds and purple. And it worked. I think most quilters today are beyond such restrictions, but still get stuck in some preconceived color schemes. Remember that any color method is only to guide you. There are multitudes of wonderful combinations. The one the rule says is wrong today will be the one newly in fashion tomorrow. So be free with color and find your own combinations.

When I first began to teach, I explained to the class all about complementary colors (opposites on the color wheel, such as orange and blue) and how to mix them to make chromatic colors. When everyone began to paint their own piece, I found that I had to go around and demonstrate mixing the complements. Students were astonished with the colors I made. So I decided it was very important for everyone to experience these mixes for themselves. Otherwise, they would never really understand how wonderful chromatic color mixes are.

In color theory, a wheel is created with the primary colors equally spaced around the rim. Red, blue, and yellow are considered the primary colors, because they cannot be mixed from any other color. On the wheel the secondary colors are placed between these three. Each is a mix of two primaries. Red and yellow make orange. Blue and yellow make green. Red and blue make violet. As you can see in Plate 2-9, that creates an arrangement where orange is directly opposite blue on the wheel. All the colors directly across from each other on the wheel are known as complementary colors. The basic three to remember are: red and green; blue and orange; yellow and violet.

If you have a color, for example an orange, which is too bright for your work, how can you tone it down? If you add black to orange you will have brown. Perhaps useful in some cases, but it is now not orange. If you add the complement of orange-blue, it will tone the brightness down and retain the hue of orange. In the following color mixing exercises we will be doing this. Mixes of

PLATE 2-8.
These are the charts I make when mixing colors. I can refer back to them when I want a particular color again.

complementary colors are referred to as chromatic colors. Since paints are pigments, pure theory differs from actuality. I use three blues and each added to orange produces a different mix. We will try all of them as the differences are quite exciting.

For all these mixes, do at least three areas. On your fabric a 1" circular sample area is all that is needed. Do three mixes – one of more blue than orange, one of equal amounts for a grayed tone, and one with more orange than blue. Look at the sample chart in Plate 2-1, page 27 to help you understand this visually. Remember to use the printed color only as a guide. Yours should be similar, but will probably be a little different from the colored chart in the photo. This variation does not matter for your learning experience.

It is helpful for later reference to put a dot of each color used in the square with their mixes. Later, while painting a landscape, you will instantly see which blue you used to achieve a particular color when you refer to the chart you are creating now. It can be confusing which blue was used. There are three different values to the blues. The darkest one is called simply blue. Some students confuse this one with the royal blue, which is the middle value and looks like the color most people think of as basic blue. If your mixes are teal – almost green – then you have used blue.

You can mix paint on the palette or on the fabric. Each gives a different look to the color. Mixed on the palette, the paint will be smoother and evenly mixed – usually. On the fabric, the paint color will be uneven and quite interesting. Try both of these methods with some of your mixing trials to observe the difference.

ROYAL BLUE AND ORANGE

Royal blue is the basic blue I use. The mixture of this blue with orange and white gives wonderful grays. Using brown, which is orange with a little black, gives very deep, dark grays. Try adding a bit of white at the bottom of your circles of mixed

PLATE 2-9.
Directly across the color wheel are the complementary colors I use for most of my mixes. When you mix two complements, they are called chromatic colors.

colors. This will show you these grays. The cliffs in many of my Mendocino quilts were painted with this combination used in varied mixes.

SKY BLUE AND ORANGE

Recently, I have been using this combination for many of my paintings. There is a green very much like the color of the ocean near Monterey that can be made with these colors. Check for it on the sample and be sure to make it as one of your samples. In my paintings the sky is usually this color with just the barest touch of orange. If you look at the real sky, it is not as blue as the sky blue paint. A bit of orange makes it the correct tone.

BLUE AND ORANGE

A wonderful teal blue or very blue green can be made with these colors. It is the green in many impressionist paintings. I just discovered this color and I am using it more. Khaki tans are on the other end of the mix with more orange in the mixture.

RED AND GREEN

The green from the jar is much too raw a color when compared to the green of trees. A little red tones it down. If you want to, you could experiment with other reds and greens. Each gives a different color. When using red and green, with the mix on the red side, adding lots of white to the mixture yields a wonderful soft purple. This is like the shadows in meadows in California. Again check the sample, look below the three basic mixes of red and green, and try to mix this lavender.

OCHER AND VIOLET

With a lot of ocher, a touch of violet, and lots of white, the golden color of California meadows can be mixed. Ocher is one of the standard colors for mixing, so even if you do not like it, you probably will find yourself using it.

GREEN AND —

Natural looking greens are hard to mix. Besides toning the green with red, I also use brown, white, or even sky blue in the mixture. Play around with these colors and others – mixing different greens so you begin to have a feel for this color. If you have mixed colors left on your palette, add these to green. Landscapes have many different greens, so this is an important color to mix.

Once you have finished all these painting exercises, you will have the basic knowledge to begin your landscape painting. The colors I have suggested are the same ones I use for most of my work. You are now ready to begin your own painting.

CHAPTER 3

OTHER PAINTING POSSIBILITIES

Rather than concerning yourself immediately with doing a landscape painting, think about making fabric for patchwork. Or play on the landscape with the following printing techniques for a more abstract landscape. Or make fabric to coordinate with your landscape. The paints handle like acrylic paints so they are very versatile. Some of the things I have tried are presented in this chapter. You probably will come up with some other ideas. Playing with the paint and different effects will be easier if you are not too concerned about the result. Experimenting is fun. Nothing will be wasted, because you can either cut it up for patchwork or paint over it.

MATERIALS:

This is a list of all the tools and materials I gathered to make the samples for this chapter. You may think of other things as you play with these techniques. Each technique has it own tools; not all of these are needed for every one. In addition to the supplies listed at the end of Chapter 1:

FABRIC

Fat quarters in white and light-colored solids for your first efforts.

PLASTIC COVERED WORK SURFACE

These methods can be messier than painting a scene.

FOR TEXTURING:

COMBS

In a variety of tooth spacings.

CRAYONS

Fabric crayons are available at art supply stores and some fabric shops. With some you draw on paper and then transfer the drawing onto fabric by ironing. These are not as intense in color as the crayons that work directly on fabric.

PENS

Permanent marking pens – black and/or colors.

FOR STAMPING AND PRINTING METHODS:

COTTON BATTING OR NEWSPAPER THE SIZE OF YOUR FABRIC

To use while printing as padding under the plastic that covers your work surface.

STAMP PAD

Pelle's or put fabric over a thin sponge, or dab paint onto stamps with a fine-grain cosmetic sponge.

BRAYER

Used instead of a stamp pad to apply the paint. Works best while doing monoprinting and vegetable printing.

FOR BLOCK PRINTING:

PAPER AND A PENCIL

To doodle designs.

PLASTIC ERASERS OR ERASER BLOCK

Art suppliers sell sheets of eraser for block printing. I found small self-stick foam sheets to cut with a scissors and apply to a wooden block and they worked very well.

LINOLEUM BLOCK CARVING TOOLS

RUBBER STAMPS

The best are those with simple shapes and deep lines.

FOUND OBJECTS

Look around the house and studio for things that have a flat surface and interesting shape.

FOR VEGETABLE PRINTING:

CABBAGE, GREEN PEPPER, CELERY, ETC.

Sliced in half or sections.

FOR POTATO PRINTING:

POTATO

KNIFE

One to cut the potato in slices and a small one for carving, or linoleum block carving tools.

FOR STENCLING:

CUTTING MAT

STRAIGHTEDGE

Triangle or ruler, for cutting straight lines.

SHARP-POINTED HOBBY KNIFE

STENCIL PAPER

STENCIL BRUSH

FOR LEAF PRINTING:

LEAVES

With interesting shapes.

BRUSHES

A soft one to brush the paint onto the leaf.

OLD TOOTHBRUSH FOR SPATTERING.

FOR MONOPRINTING:

SHEET OF GLASS

Large enough for what you wish to print. Tape edge, back with white cardboard, or use your tabletop if washable.

FEATHERS

Can be used to paint onto the glass.

RUBBER STAMPS, PALETTE KNIFE, ETC.

Things to press into the paint or draw in the paint.

USING PAINTED FABRIC

Very exciting patchwork blocks can be created using fabric you have painted yourself. This really individualizes your work. Whenever I need to make a block as a gift, I try to put some of my painted fabric into it. Sponging, stippling, and spattering over a loosely painted ground color all give great results; or start with a colored fabric. With all the techniques I am presenting, you can make fabric to piece or appliqué.

PLATE 3-1.

All the things I gathered, along with those in Plate 3-12, to do block printing, texturing, stamping, and stenciling.

DESIGNING FABRIC

For most of these methods very simple designs work best. The interest in them is in the repetition of pattern. Do some doodling and chose a simple design based on one of the basic shapes in Figure 3-1. Then try it out with one of the techniques below. You will learn a lot with your first attempts.

Once you have a design it can be randomly printed or printed in a repeat pattern. There are basic patterns used for design repeats in fabric design (see Figure 3-2). These are usually based on simple shapes (see Figure 3-1). Since you will be doing custom hand work, you can stamp any pattern, but it may be simpler to begin designing with these basic shapes and repeats. The same repeats can be laid on top of each other for more layers of design. If you are familiar with quilting designs, you can use the same repeat patterns for your stamping – rows, alternating, mirror image, forty-five degree turns, etc. This gives you a beginning. You can invent your own or do random stamping.

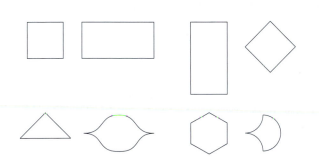

FIGURE 3-1 (LEFT).
Basic shapes for repeats. From these basic shapes, many patterns can be made. Cut your block (potato, eraser, etc.) into one of these and then cut a design into the shape. Play around with repeats of this design.

FIGURE 3-2 (BELOW).
Standard repeat patterns. A few of the repeats used in fabric designing.

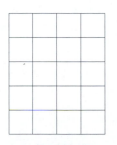

A. Equal Blocks

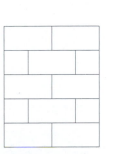

B. Brick – one half-step

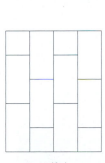

C. Half-drop

D. Diamond

E. Triangle

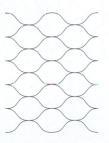

F. Ogee

G. Hexagons

H. Clam Shells

PLATE 3-2.
Background fabric can be made easily by sponging a color over the entire piece of fabric. This sponged fabric was used to back my dolphin stenciling.

BACKGROUND FABRIC

Having a painted ground to use for stamping or stenciling can make the finished fabric more exciting. Just about any method can work, but three I've tried are sponging, scrunching, and plastic-wrap printing. My samples were exciting as they were, so these can also be used just for making fabric. For sponging, I used a large holey sponge, sometimes called a seawool. After wetting the sponge, using the paint rather wet, I dipped the sponge into the paint and pressed it onto the fabric repeatedly all over. This then became the background for my dolphin stenciling (see Plate 3-2).

For scrunching, I actually scrunched up fabric in a wad on top of my plastic. Then I used a large sponge quite wet to press paint onto the fabric. I used several mixes of blue to have a range of color. It was left to dry overnight. When I opened it the next morning, it had a tie-dyed look (see Plate 3-3).

The plastic-wrap printing was done by wrapping plastic wrap over a piece of cardboard about

PLATE 3-3.
Fabric can be scrunched up and sponged over with wet paint to achieve this almost tie-dyed effect. I applied several colors to give the color more depth.

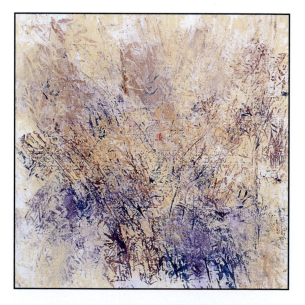

PLATE 3-4.
Wrapping a piece of cardboard with plastic wrap and then painting it with a brush makes an interesting stamp. I was trying to create a meadow effect that I intended to stamp with flowers, but this is nice as it is.

4" x 6". I worked the plastic into folds and then taped it on the back with some left for me to use as a handle. Then I painted colors onto the plastic with a wide brush and pressed it onto the fabric. I was trying to make meadow effects and used meadow colors (see Plate 3-4). This is the same technique I used to texture the meadow of my BARN AT SUNSET (see Plate 11-3, page 126). After painting the meadow with colors, I textured over them with the plastic-wrap technique.

SILKSCREEN

Versatex™ and Createx™ were developed to be silkscreened. This is the method commercial printers use. Screens are available for the individual craftsperson at art supply stores. In silkscreening, the paint is pressed through a stretched screen with a stencil on it. Even though the concept is simple, there are many variations. I am not going to go into detail on this process. I just wanted to mention it as a possibility to explore and for those already familiar with silkscreening. There are many good books available to guide you.

TEXTURING

Just about any of the techniques painters use for texturing can be adapted to fabric painting. An example of this is in Ardis Naur Normanly's "TIL SKOVBRYNGAARD" (see Plate 3-5). She drew lines with the handle end of her paintbrush to give interesting texture to the hair in her painting. When I was in art school, we often scraped the paint off with our brush ends.

This same thing could be done with other tools. Toothpicks, sticks from trees, palette knives— all would work. Combs also make interesting lines in the paint and come in many different widths. Collect some of these items and play with them.

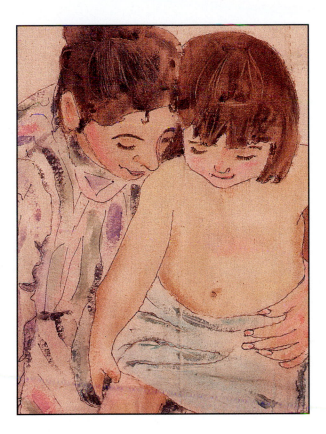

PLATE 3-5 (ABOVE).
"TIL SKOVBRYNGAARD," detail, 24" x 26", Ardis Naur Normanly. Aromas, California, 1988. In a private collection on the island of Møn, Denmark. Photo by Pat Cullins Monahan. After: Mary Cassatt (1844–1926), The Bath (La Toilette) 1891. The hair in Ardis's quilt is particularly well done. She scraped away the paint in the direction of the hair with the stick end of her paint brush, giving it a lovely texture.

PLATE 3-6 (RIGHT).
For this example of texturizing with a comb, I first dropped thick wet paint all over the fabric. Then I drew a comb through the paint in a wavy motion.

PLATE 3-7.

To do this rubbing with fabric crayons, I first arranged children's blocks in the pattern I wanted. Then I placed the fabric over the blocks. Using the crayon in a loose one-direction motion, and holding the fabric in place, I colored over them until I liked the result.

PLATE 3-8.

HENNING HANSEN'S 70TH BIRTHDAY, detail 15" x 21", Ardis Naur Normanly, Aromas, California, 1988. In a private collection on the island of Møn, Denmark. Photo by Pat Cullins Monahan. From: Salinas Rodeo photo cover of California Living *magazine of San Francisco,* Sunday Examiner Chronicle, *July 1, 1979, photo by: Nick Paoloff. In this detail, you can see how Ardis used a marking pen to draw the scene and then colored it with the paints.*

FABRIC CRAYONS

There are two different types of crayons for use on fabric. One is used by drawing on paper and ironing the paper image onto fabric. Another type can be used directly on the fabric. You can actually draw directly on the fabric with either, but the ones made to do this give a stronger color. The crayons can be used in conjunction with the paint either wet or dry. This gives another interesting texture to combine with the paint. In my experimenting, rubbing gave me the most exciting results. Using an old set of children's blocks with raised letters, I placed the fabric over them and rubbed the crayon on the fabric. The raised areas then appeared on the fabric in the color used. Look around you, many things have raised areas. Textured sections can be just as interesting as my letters.

MARKING PENS

The easiest way to do any writing on your quilts is with a felt-tip marking pen. When I noticed on one of my early quilts that the signature had badly faded, but the rest was fine, it greatly concerned me. I began testing all the pens I could find to see which ones would not fade. Using each pen, I wrote its name on a muslin fabric, covered half of the writing with cardboard and put the whole thing out in the summer sun for three days and then washed it. This exposure to light was much longer than that used to test commercial dyes. Most of the pens I purchased as permanent fabric markers in fabric stores were quite permanent. In my test the only one that did fade was the one I used for several years to sign my name. It is always best to do a test of your materials. I now sign my name with the Pilot®-SC-UF pen, because it does not bleed and it has a good thickness of line. Which pen to use would be based on the line thickness desired among those I tested. To assure the permanence of your marking pen, be sure to heat-set it with an iron.

Another use for the pens would be to combine them with the paints in creating your landscape. Ardis Naur Normanly does a drawing and then washes color over the drawing. That is one way to use them. You can also do the painting first and then draw the line work on top.

BLOCK PRINTING

There are many variations on block printing. The idea is to have something you can ink and stamp on the fabric repeatedly. Some of the possibilities are rubber stamps, eraser stamps, found objects, vegetables, and potato stamps. Once you have the idea, you will come up with some of your own.

I have used three ways to apply the paint to the block. If you have a roller called a brayer, it is easier to apply the paint onto the block for some of these methods. Brayers are available at art supply stores along with linoleum block printing tools. It is possible to use a linoleum block with the fabric paints, but other materials work better. The paint has a water base and tends to bead on the linoleum.

PLATE 3-9. *ASILOMAR REVISITED, 19" x 20½", Lois Pio, Hermosa Beach, California, ©1990. Private collection. Photo by Susan Einstein. The kelp is a linoleum block that Lois had cut some years ago. Lois used her hand-dyed fabrics to do the border for her quilt. The shells were collected from the beach at Asilomar.*

PLATE 3-10.
Letters are available in rubber stamps so you can write on your quilt. These were in the children's section of my art supply store and were very inexpensive. A quick way to apply the paint to the stamp is to brush it on. There is a texture left when you stamp, but it is quite nice.

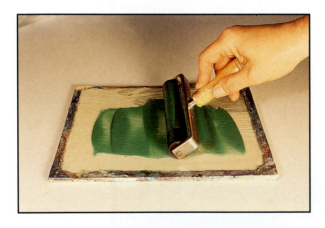

PLATE 3-11.
Another way to put paint on large blocks is with a brayer. Spread paint on a smooth surface such as glass or plastic with the brayer until it is evenly covered. Then roll the brayer over the block. This applies the paint very evenly over large surfaces.

To apply paint to a block, spread the paint out on plastic or a piece of glass with the brayer. Once it transfers evenly to the brayer in an area as large as your block, roll the paint onto the block with the brayer. An alternate method is to brush the paint onto the block. This covers unevenly and shows brush strokes, but is interesting. You must be careful to not leave paint built up on the edges of the block. Rather than rolling or brushing the paint on, the block itself can be pressed into the paint. A stamp pad, which works particularly well with most methods, is sold by Pelle's. It has a pad made from a fine-grain sponge so details still print well. A pad can be made with felt or a thin sponge wrapped with fabric. A fine-grain cosmetic sponge can be used the same way as a pad, but tapped onto the block.

Printing with padding underneath the fabric can help you obtain a better image. Professional printing tables have a rubber pad which does not give much, but has a bit of resilience. It is somewhat like inner tube material. Pads of newspapers or batting with plastic over them can substitute. In all the printing methods, smooth fabric will give a clearer image.

Printing blocks can be made from any material that has a somewhat flat face to press onto the fabric. For one block, I glued matchsticks to a piece of cardboard with white glue. Another time, I cut cardboard shapes and put a cardboard handle on them. Pasta can be glued onto cardboard for interesting forms. Felt also works when cut into shapes and glued to cardboard. The glue you use should not soften with water once it has hardened. Otherwise, your pieces will loosen when you print with the waterbase paints.

RUBBER STAMPS

An easy and fun technique to use with the paints is rubber stamping. You can purchase stamps or make your own. Look for simple, bold designs and deeply incised lines, as very detailed ones do not work well on fabric. This is another time for testing before working on a finished project. Any line drawing, one which is done with black lines or dots, can be made into a rubber stamp. Most rubber stamp companies and some small printers offer this service inexpensively. Blocks made with erasers are also "rubber stamps."

Carving erasers into stamps works especially well. The paint does not bead up on an eraser like it does on linoleum, so it makes a better block printing tool. Carving your own images gives you great freedom to design. They are available immediately and are quite sturdy, too. You can purchase stamp-making kits from rubber stamp companies.

In my experience the best erasers to carve are plastic ones. Some erasers crumble when carved, but plastic erasers cut smoothly with little effort. The best designs for erasers are bold and simple. Silhouettes work well. You can incise some lines into a shape for detail. Leaving thin lines of eraser is difficult. Large sheets of material similar to plastic erasers can be purchased from mail-order art suppliers for larger stamps.

Once you have your design, lay tracing paper over it and trace with a very soft pencil (6B). Put the tracing face down onto the eraser and carefully press it down. This should transfer the drawing to the eraser. You can touch up the drawing with a pen if it is necessary.

The tools sold to carve linoleum blocks work well on the eraser. Sharp-pointed knives also carve well. I found it best to first trace around the shape with a sharp-pointed hobby knife, making sure I did not undercut the image. Then I used the wide curved carving blade to cut away the unwanted background of the eraser. After most of it was gone, I used the V-shaped carving blade to cut away the rest of the background. For incised lines, the smallest V-shaped blade worked well. As a final step you may want to cut the eraser into the shape of the carved image so the background does not bend and print.

The paint can be applied to the stamps with a brush, but because most stamps are small, it works better to use a stamp pad. You apply the paint to

PLATE 3-12.
Erasers are easy to carve and make good stamps for fabric. Here are several types that work, but the white plastic eraser was the easiest to carve. The large white block is a similar material sold in larger sizes. Linoleum block carving tools work well and are available through most art suppliers. If your stamp leaves unwanted marks from the background when you print, remove the background from around the image as I did from the fish stamp.

PLATE 3-13.
For this design I cut a piece of eraser block into a rectangle (see Plate 3-12, upper right top). Then I drew lines on it to make angled shapes. The lines were cut with a hobby knife and then the background was cleared away with the curved linoleum block carving tool. Rows of light blue were printed in the scattered brick pattern. On top, darker blue rows were printed – offset one-half step down and to the side. The block was inked with Pelle's stamp pad.

the pad with a tool such as a palette knife and smooth it out. Then gently tap the stamp into the paint several times. Press the stamp to the fabric with hard pressure. The more detailed and larger stamps seem to take more pressure, so really lean into them with your body weight. You will have a good image without paint built up on or in the edges. Pads can be made with fabric-covered felt or flat sponges. The best pad I have found is available from Pelle's. It is made from a very fine-grain sponge, which gives excellent detail. The sponge can be rinsed out after each working session and reused. Pelle's sends you several so you can have several colors in use.

You can use paint from the jars diluted to the consistency of very thick cream. This dilutes the color however, so airbrush inks may be a better choice if you are doing a lot of stamping. They give a more intense color. The inks are already the correct consistency, so you can pour them directly on the pad. Most of my samples were done with paint from a jar.

While working you can wipe the stamps with nonalcoholic baby wipes or wet paper towels. When you are finished working, clean your stamps with a toothbrush under running water. I use my stamps only with fabric or water-base paint so there is no difficulty with ink residue transferring onto the fabric. Some stamps should not be cleaned with the alcohol-based cleaners that are necessary with some inks. So, be alert to your stamp's requirements if you do use anything but water-base paint.

The stamps can be used to make a colored image or an outline. If you stamp an outline, the

PLATE 3-14.
LOG CABIN, 8" x 8", Pele Fleming, Davenport, California, 1992.
OCEAN WAVES, 6½" x 6½", Pele Fleming, Davenport, California, 1994.
STARS AND BOATS, 6¼" x 6¼", Pele Fleming, Davenport, California, 1993.
Many exciting images are available on rubber stamps or you can have one made. Pele Fleming makes them from quilt block patterns and stamps miniature quilts, which she then colors with felt-tip permanent pens.

inside of the image can then be colored with dilute paint. Heat-set the stamped paint with an iron before painting over the stamped image to help keep it from bleeding. You can stamp in black or brown and then color the image with felt-tip markers. Remember to heat-set the colored image, also.

Rubber stamps are an exciting way to use multiple images for designing. Start playing with the stamps and using them together. They can be used to make fabric, as elements of design in a quilt, or to stamp a complete quilt. There are many creative possibilities with the stamps on fabric.

Variations on Blocks

At my art supply store I found, in the children's section, sheets of self-adhesive foam material to make blocks for stamping. After cutting the material with scissors it is pressed onto wooden blocks. It is a very simple method for making blocks and works very well. I used Pelle's pad to ink the blocks. Look around your art supply store and see what you can find. Often simple materials in the children's section work quite well.

Found Objects

Found objects make interesting blocks. I have a potato masher which has never mashed a potato, but makes great printed shapes. While doing samples for this book I looked around my sewing studio and found some great objects. Gently pressed into a Pelle's stamp pad, bobbins, spools, thimbles, beeswax holders, and buttons all made great impressions. Look around you with this in mind and you will be surprised at what you may find to try printing.

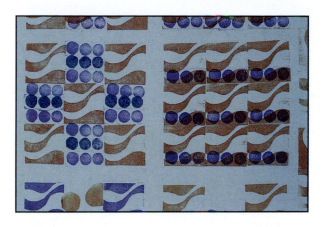

Plate 3-15.
These designs were made with the same two blocks that were created from self-stick sheets of foam cut with scissors and pressed to a wooden block. The circles were in a row of three, so for the top pattern three rows were printed. Pelle's stamp pad was used to ink the blocks.

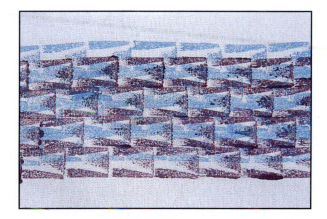

Plate 3-16.
This stamping was done with my open-toe presser foot inked with Pelle's stamp pad. Rows of blue were stamped and then rows of maroon over the blue, but offset.

Plate 3-17 (right).
This is stamped with a beeswax holder, bobbins, and the end of spools, all of which were inked with Pelle's stamp pad.

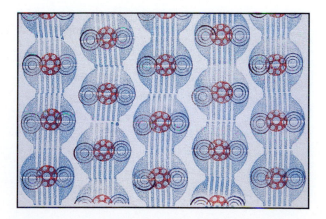

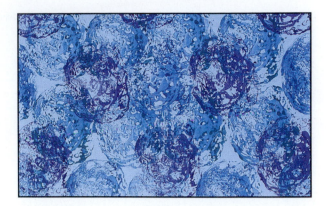

PLATE 3-18.
Very interesting prints can be made with different vegetables. Some need to be dried a bit before printing as they have a high water content. This one was done with a cabbage. The sliced cabbage was inked with a brayer and printed in three different colors.

PLATE 3-19.
Potatoes can be carved into simple shapes and used to print. It helps to let potatoes dry a bit before printing. This fish design used the full round of the sliced potato. A brayer was used to ink the potato stamp.

VEGETABLE PRINTING

Vegetables can be sliced and used to print. After I bought several different vegetables just for this purpose, my husband looked into the refrigerator and said, "Well, puppies, even the refrigerator is part of Vicki's quilting now." For applying the paint to the vegetables, I found the brayer worked best.

POTATO STAMPING

Potatoes can be carved in many shapes and used to print. Potatoes can be kept a short time in the refrigerator, but have a limited life. This keeps you from building up a collection of designs, but they are simple and cheap blocks. Cut the potato into one of the basic shapes, and then freely carve into it with a knife or block carving tools. These need to be very simple designs. The brayer or pad work best for inking potato blocks.

STENCILING

Another very easy method to make shapes is with stenciling. It is the opposite approach to block printing. A hole is made for the design and then paint is applied through the hole. I found stenciling paper best to use. It is inexpensive and available at art suppliers. Other things, such as plastic sheet protectors or heavy paper or even quilter's template plastic, work too. If you want to reuse your stencil many times, plastic is best. Use a sharp-pointed knife on top of a piece of cardboard or your cutting mat. If you make complicated designs, remember to connect the holes with narrow bridges so the stencil stays together. There is a world of stencils available if you do not want to make your own. Quilting templates are a possibility, also.

Stippling with stiff stenciling brushes is the traditional method for applying the paint. They work

PLATE 3-20 (LEFT).
These dolphins were stenciled on top of fabric I had already sponged with sky blue paint. After it was dry I stenciled in two steps — the top and bottom of the dolphins were two different stencils.

best, but you can also use a sponge or toothbrush. Spattering over the stencil is effective, too. Taping the stencil in place helps prevent it from moving. Load the stiff stenciling brush by tapping it into the paint. Then clean the excess off by tapping it onto the palette or scrap fabric until the brush gives you the texture you want. (Traditionally this is a very soft small-dotted texture which looks good, but I use more paint for most of mine.) Then tap the brush over the openings in the stencil until the fabric is covered as you want it. Remove the stencil carefully and clean it with paper towels. Be sure to check the back if you have stenciled over another painted area, so you do not transfer paint onto still another area.

This same technique works in reverse. Paint a shape cut from stencil paper or plastic template material. Then press the painted shape onto the fabric. That shape or a design painted onto the plastic can be used.

PLATE 3-22.
Spattering over the leaf is another way to print.

PLATE 3-21.
In this palm tree stencil sample different colors were applied to the same stencil for color variation – from the leaves to the trunk of the tree. Less color was applied to the top trees, so they appear farther away.

PLATE 3-23.
Brush the paint onto a leaf and then use it to stamp. These Japanese maple leaves were placed randomly and are particularly effective.

LEAF PRINTS

Both the block printing method and stenciling can be used with leaves or other natural objects. Maple leaves work especially well. Brush the paint onto the leaf and lay it onto the fabric. Then cover it with paper towel and press. The towel absorbs any excess paint and keeps it from running onto the fabric. Or, lay the leaf on the fabric and spatter the paint around it, using the leaf to create a space. (See Plates 3-22 and 3-23.)

MONOPRINTS

If you have tried the painting, you probably have discovered the paint transfers easily from the painted plastic or other surface to the fabric. This can be used as a printing method. It only allows one print, but many artists find it an exciting tech-nique. It is very simple. Paint onto a hard surface such as plastic or glass. Then lay the fabric carefully onto the paint. Press it with your hand or a clean brayer. If there is heavy paint you must be careful not to press too hard and smear the design. Lift the fabric carefully from the paint and put it aside to dry. Sometimes several impressions can be made, but each is softer.

Once you are familiar with the paints and begin to look for ways to use them, you will come up with even more methods. All the techniques can be used in combination. Being able to apply paint to the fabric instead of using more elaborate dye lets you try almost any of the techniques artists have been developing. The simplest things seem to work best and allow you to be the most creative. Keep your mind and eyes open and have fun.

PLATE 3-24.
Ree Nancarrow spread paint with a brayer onto a Formica table. Then she used different tools to create designs in the paint. Most were done with the edge of a palette knife. Photo by Pat Cullins Monahan.

SECTION II

CREATING A
PAINTED AND PATCHED
WALL QUILT

CHAPTER 4

PAINTING A LANDSCAPE

The next chapters give directions for creating a wall quilt, using a landscape as the example. I photographed a small quilt at each stage of construction, so you can see it progress. There is a drawing included (Figure 4-3, page 55) if you wish to try the same scene used in the sample quilt, but I encourage you to paint something important to you.

In addition to the materials you gathered to do the painting exercises, you will need the following to do your own landscape painting:

SLIDE OR PHOTOGRAPH

Your favorite landscape.

FABRIC

A piece of fabric 2" longer and 2" wider than your desired painting. For instance, if you want a finished painting of 12" x 15" cut or tear a piece of fabric 14" x 17". This allows for seams and fraying in the washing machine and allows room for changes (Figure 4-1).

PAINT

A selection of colors you want to use.

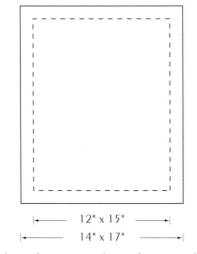

12" x 15"
14" x 17"

This is the size for painting with extra for seams and fraying.

12½" x 15½"

Draw this cutting line lightly with pencil onto fabric.

FIGURE 4-1 (RIGHT).
Preparing fabric for painting. When cutting fabric for painting, be sure to allow extra for seams and fraying.

SELECTING A SUBJECT

Nature offers a rich source of inspiration for painting and designing. From distant views to very close-up details, nature is endlessly inspiring. It is best to use a scene very familiar to you. Knowing how something looks from all sides or in different lighting enhances the finished artwork. If you are using a piece of driftwood, examining its texture and feeling its smooth ridges will improve your painting. If you can visit the location and hold the objects while you are painting, this will add even more. When you are trying to paint a place very familiar to you, you will notice things you never needed to know before. Working from photos or slides is a practical way to make notes about the subject. Having more than one view available gives you even more information to draw on. Gather as many pictures as you can, even postcards, of the subject. Even if you are not doing the particular angle on the postcard, it may give you a better roof line than the view you are using. At the very least, different photos will help you understand the subject better.

Observing the lighting at a particular time of day may be important for your painting. I did many quilts of Mendocino, but some were at different times of the day or season. It helped my paintings to be aware of the colors and shading created by the time chosen. It can be exciting to discover an effect you had not observed before. When I was painting MENDOCINO FOGBANK (Plate 11-2, page 126), I was not consciously aware that the fog was purple or pink. I found when I went to paint it, that I made it purple. Then I went out and checked. Evidently, living on the coast and seeing the fog, my right brain remembered.

If you cannot do this kind of direct observation, it will be important to paint a subject very familiar to you. If you have never been to the place, you may not know whether a shadow is a tree or a path. How you decide to paint it can be affected by that knowledge.

When selecting a scene to paint, pick one that is simple for your first effort. Also, look for one having something in it that gives it scale. This can be a building or fence or an animal or people. However, the form selected should also be simple because some objects are more difficult to paint. I have suggested painting a landscape because landscapes are forgiving of mistakes. A misshaped hill still looks like a hill, even if it is not quite like the original. People, in particular, must have the correct shape. Silhouetted beachwalkers appear in many of my beach scenes and are simple to paint because they are small, but they add the necessary interest and scale. You can see this in the example painting. Detailed forest scenes may have many difficult-to-paint details, but very little to indicate scale. A redwood tree only becomes gigantic when a person stands next to it.

Buildings and manmade objects are great candidates for appliqué. You can try painting them, but can later cover any unsuccessful areas with appliqué. Or use a combination as I often do. That helps connect the painted portion of the quilt with the appliquéd portion.

Many beginners try to use photos of other people's paintings. This can be done, but I think a few things should be kept in mind. If entering a competition or exhibition, the original artist should be

PLATE 4-1. *WILD ROSES, detail, 24" x 33", Vicki L. Johnson, Soquel, California, © 1993. A combination of painting and appliqué, as on this building, can be quite effective.*

acknowledged. Ardis Naur Normanly has used Mary Cassatt's work and acknowledges her.

It is a good learning experience to copy another artist's work, but you are copying. Using your own technique, as Ardis did, would be better for exhibiting. That way you have interpreted the work, not just copied it. Such a quilt might be appropriate in a guild quilt show, but not in a larger competition.

For a first effort, it is easiest to work from a photograph of an actual scene familiar to you. The students who work from paintings seem to have more difficulty. They struggle to match the same colors and technique as the painting. These can only be matched using the same media. Fabric paints react differently than the more traditional media. It would be best to learn how they work first.

THOUGHTS ON CREATING

Keep in mind that everything I say is a suggestion only. I encourage you to experiment and to try your own ideas. As soon as rules are set, a creative person will come along and show that doing it just the opposite way works beautifully.

Make some observations about how you work. Everyone has a different working style. Some artists work early in the morning and others stay up all night. Some are very messy and others must have everything in its proper place. Do not buy into the clichés about creative people. The only constants I have observed are the differences. This extends into how you approach the painting process. Identifying your own working rhythm will help you actually do the work. Once the original enthusiasm begins to wane and problems arise, everyone begins to procrastinate even if they really want to do the painting. Creating also takes discipline. Knowing yourself and how you best work will help you through the harder parts of creating.

TIPS ON THE PAINTING

Study the examples shown in this book and you will begin to see how simple each scene actually is. We are creating an illusion of a landscape, not a photographic likeness. A little detail added at the end can make it seem quite realistic. Loose painterly areas for the main body of the painting add to the richness.

Look at an area of the fabric when it is wet. Even on the white plastic it will look dark. Keep in mind that the water wetting the fabric makes the colors look darker. I let an area dry before deciding whether it is too dark. The amount of water in the paint will affect the value more than using heavier paint, but until they dry an area with heavy paint and an area with diluted paint may appear very close in value. A thin coat of paint on a warm day in dry weather will probably dry in one hour. The time required varies with the temperature, humidity, and amount of water and paint used. Hanging the painting outside will help it dry faster, but the wet areas will run more if it is hung. Snapping clothespins on the bottom edge of a hung painting will help keep it from blowing in the wind and flipping up onto itself. You can use a hair dryer to speed the drying.

Studying your work from a distance is very important. If you only look at it close up while painting, you cannot see the overall value relationships. Prop your work up and stand back at different distances. Squint when you look or if nearsighted, remove your glasses. This blurs the detail so you see what stands out and what recedes. There are reducing glasses available (similar to magnifying glasses) which also help you see the work in a different perspective. Another trick to get a fresh look is to put it in front of a mirror.

When I make a quilt 24" x 30", it takes me an average of 22 hours. Knowing this may help you pace yourself. Usually, I do three of this size at a time. That way I can paint on one while another one is drying.

SIZES

For all my work, I use a module of three inches. This means in a finished quilt all the squares are 3" squares. I think in terms of the completed work and add seam allowances later. Figure 4-2, shows a module and several multiples of it that I have used. My favorite results in a quilt 24" x 30". From now on if I mention sizes, I will be working toward a quilt of this size. If you choose to work on a different size, adjust the measurements.

It is necessary to select a module size before beginning to paint so all the parts will fit together without needing major adjustment. For a large piece this is especially important. I do a thumbnail sketch for the basic layout before beginning. If needed, I work out the proportions on graph paper. For a diagram of suggested small quilt layouts, see Figure 6-1, page 80.

I allow extra fabric while doing the painting in case I like an area on the edge enough to change the cropping. With enough extra, I can even lengthen the work three inches.

DESIGN PRINCIPLES

All the principles of design you have learned in making quilts apply to painting as well. Design is design no matter what the medium.

A composition with unequal emphasis is more interesting. For example, put the focal point off center or the horizon line above or below center. Let one thing dominate – let one thing be the biggest, the brightest, the darkest, the most complex.

Too many complex elements are overkill. For instance, doing sponge work on everything is too busy. It is rather like too many same-size calico prints. One or two elements with this texture are enough.

In perspective, the distant objects are paler, bluer, and simpler. You can see this in the trees and hills in the distance. Building the washes from light to dark and loose to detailed also suggests perspective.

Pick a base color for most of your work. Mixing the colors, you have learned how one blue changes when mixed with orange. Many different gray values can be made. An interesting challenge is to do a painting using only two complementary colors and black and white. Having one basic blue helps to

hold the piece together and gives it a color tone. Adding other blues in smaller quantities does help to make it richer. With quilts, this color principle is true also. They must have a color tone that predominates for the design to work.

Think in terms of three basic values to achieve forms such as hills or cliffs – light, dark, and middle tones. Leave the fabric or use very light paint for the forward areas, the darkest paint for the receding or deepest ones, and middle values for the rest. Once you have reduced the form to the basic values, it should begin to round. Variations in tone or color can be glazed over the form.

DRAWING

If you want a realistic scene, drawing from memory is difficult. Most artists use sketches, photos, or clippings to give them something to look at when they cannot work directly from the model or scene. (Graphic designers refer to their collections of clippings as scrap.) For most of my work I take slides of the scene I wish to paint. Painting fabric at the site is not as easy as with traditional media like watercolor. It is possible, but I have not done it. I do have books and several binders full of clippings, postcards, and pictures of the things I like to use.

I project a slide onto either the fabric or a piece of paper. Then I draw what I want of the scene, just making the basic shapes. This is where the artist

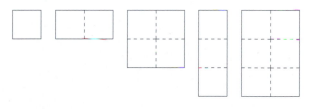

FIGURE 4-2.
Modules of a three-inch square. These are some of the shapes made using a three-inch square. It would also be modular to begin cutting the square into smaller shapes, such as a 1½" square or a 1½" x 3" rectangle.

PLATE 4-2.
To do the drawing for the example, I worked from this photograph of the beach at Mackerricher Beach State Park, Mendocino County, California. This is a good scene for beginners to try, so I have included the drawing for it (Figure 4-3). You have my permission to have this color-copied for your personal use. As you can see, I cropped it for the example. However, if you look at BEACHWALK I used a different composition and colors. See Plates 4-3 (page 56) and 9-6 (page 113). You may want to try a different area of the photo, but the people on the beach give it scale and are necessary for this scene to work well.

FIGURE 4-3A AND 4-3B (RIGHT).
BEACHWALKERS drawing. You may copy this drawing and enlarge it on a copy machine for your own use if you want to try doing this scene. The top drawing gives the basic shapes you need to trace onto fabric. The bottom drawing gives more detail.

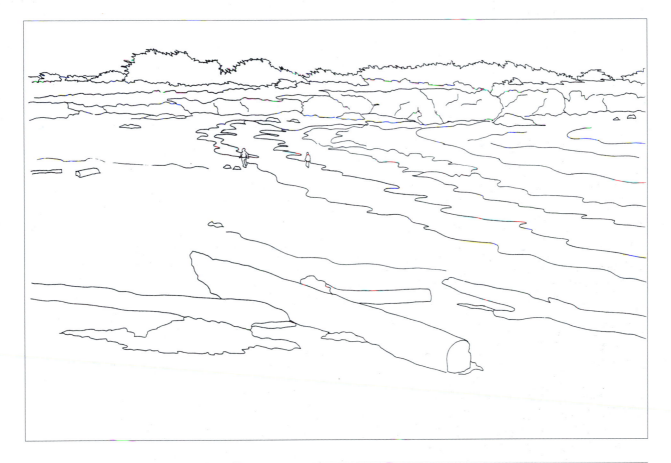

begins to make selections. Elements have to be simplified or eliminated. For example, hills in the background can have many color changes and it is hard to discern what is color variation and what is another hill. Knowing the scene well helps. Trace only the major shapes.

If drawing on fabric I use a soft No. 2 pencil. Some of these drawn lines may show through in the painting, but I consider the drawing an integral part of the work and do not concern myself with that. When drawing on paper I may first draw with a pencil, but then retrace the lines with a black felt-tip pen, usually one of my Pilot® SC-UF pens. Then the black lines can be seen through the fabric so they can be traced again.

You can also work directly from a photograph. Again, I recommend using a scene that is familiar to you or at least one where you have been. Having seen an area in many light and weather changes will help with the painting. I often return to the scene while working on a painting to help me see again what I am attempting to paint. If you have never painted before, you will be surprised at how intently and perhaps differently, it helps you to see. Many students have told me it changed their way of looking at landscape and they were delighted.

Have you really looked at fog? What color is it? White? It can be lavender or pink depending on the location of the sun. Did you know there are purple trees? In Los Angeles, the streets of the older sections are lined with them in spring. This is the type of surprise really looking at things can give. We tend to have learned clichés about what we expect to see. One of the most important lessons taught in art schools is how to see. Once your eye can see without expectations, you can create and paint better.

PLATE 4-3. *BEACHWALK, 42" x 48", Vicki L. Johnson, Mendocino, California, © 1985. Collection of Mountain Bell, Denver, Colorado. Photo by George R. Young. Without the two suggested people on the beach, there would be nothing to give this painting scale and it would not be successful. I have done several versions of this scene in many sizes.*

If the photograph is small, put a piece of tracing paper over it and using a soft pencil trace the outline of the basic forms you see. Try to not press hard or you will indent the photo. Retrace the lines on the paper with a black pen. With a copy machine, enlarge the tracing to the size you wish to paint. If it does not go large enough, you can enlarge the copy – even doing it in parts.

Once you have the tracing of the photo the size you want, you can lay the fabric over it and trace with a pencil. If you cannot see because the lines are not dark enough or the fabric too thick, either use a light box or the window. By taping the paper to the window and the fabric on top, you have a makeshift light box.

If you do have a light box, a color copy can be used to do the tracing. Placed on the box, it is surprisingly easy to see the forms. MeSewCo makes an inexpensive light box that works well for this purpose. Color copies are inexpensive to make 11" x 17" and can be done from photos or slides. Even if you do not use the color copy to directly draw on the fabric, it makes it easier to follow your photo since everything is enlarged.

It may seem like more work to first work on paper, but I have found I often wish to repeat the same scene. The paper pattern allows me to redo the painting as many times as I want. Often I will do a foggy version and a sunny one. They never turn out exactly the same and this is interesting.

Sometimes students seem to feel this procedure is cheating and they should be able to draw the scene themselves. Drawing is a skill that anyone who wants to can learn. It will help your design abilities to study drawing, but you do not have to be able to draw to design. In the end it is what you do with the work and not how you got there. If Raphael had had slide projectors and copy machines, he probably would have used them. Contemporary artists are using everything available to them and they should. This influence will be a part of the art of our time just as the influence of the science of mathematics was on the Renaissance.

CROPPING

You are in control of the cropping. What you choose to paint of a scene is part of the design. Just because a slide or photo is made to a certain size, you do not have to do the complete picture. Cut two L-shaped pieces of paper. Place them on the photo at opposite corners and move them around to frame different parts of the picture. This is a way to try different compositions. Remember, you can paint in more than is in the photo. The easiest example is the sky. With more sky the composition may be better.

APPROACHES

When starting a painting, it is sometimes overwhelming to think about doing the complete picture. You need to break it down into sections, both actually and in your mind. For instance, if I think about painting one of my big Mendocino paintings in its entirety, I can become quite discouraged. What a lot of work! Where do I start? So I think first of the sky. Is it a foggy day or a sunny one? Then I paint that area. This begins to establish

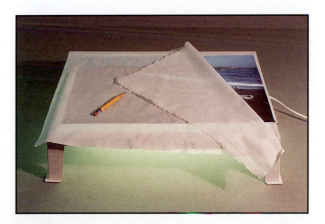

PLATE 4-4.
Another way to draw the basic scene onto fabric is to have a color copy made. Most copy shops can make them from photos or slides and enlarge them to 11" x 17" (or even larger in steps, but it is cheaper to have a black and white drawing enlarged if you want to go bigger). Place the color copy on a light box with the fabric over it. You should be able to see the basic shapes well enough to trace the outlines.

color values I must keep in mind for the next space. The more traditional approach is to paint light and distant areas first, then the dark areas and last the details. Experience and a little thinking ahead will help you decide which approach to use. Try it the traditional way first until experience gives you other ideas.

By breaking the painting into sections, you can concentrate on the part in front of you. It must be related to the complete work, but can be thought about alone. With complicated works or for beginners, this is especially helpful.

When painting a landscape I work from the top down. I paint the sky first because it is at the top and when doing it first I will not be reaching over wet paint. It is also usually done with very wet runny paint, so I want that layer on first. Heavier or

darker paint can be painted over the lighter sky once it is dry. Then I go to an area separate from the sky, such as the cliffs or meadow. The looser, wetter parts are again painted in these areas. Next is probably the ocean. Once adjacent areas are dry, I paint that area. Even on smaller paintings I work in several sessions. Painting is very tiring work because it requires high concentration. One and one-half hours is a good working session; during the time between working sessions the paint can dry.

When there is some paint on an area like the cliffs, you can do sponge work on top to give added texture. It is best to have a little color underneath to give a general tone to that space. All the texturing techniques – sponging, spattering, stippling – are best on top of color, either paint or colored fabric.

Putting a color down and then mixing another

PLATE 4-5A.

STEP 1. *For this scene, I first painted the sky with a very wet wash of sky blue and a tiny, tiny bit of orange. It was applied unevenly, allowing the paint to run together. Then the sand was painted with a mixture of approximately 40% white, 10% brown, 10% royal blue, 2% red, and 2% orange. (The percentages are approximate and used only to give you an idea of how I reached this particular color.) If you look at the photo of this scene, you will notice that the sand is not really this color. I use the photo only as a guide. The sand color was applied wet, but not as wet as the sky, with the one-inch wide brush in random strokes so it would remain splotchy. White was added to the color for the central area. For the shadows on the sand, I added more royal blue and did them while the other sand was still wet so the edges bled and were softer, which seems more realistic. Then I painted the waves with white pearlescent used with very little water. By this time the sky color had stopped bleeding and begun to dry. It had not bled into the meadow area very much, so I decided I could paint it next. The meadow color was mixed as approximately 50% white, 25% ocher, and some of the leftover sand shadow color. I could also have used violet, but I liked the soft purple of the leftover color and had quite a lot of it. Each area painted at this beginning stage is separated by some other space which will be painted a darker color. This way it does not matter if the paint bleeds into its neighbor, so it can be used very wet with no extender. All this was allowed to dry overnight before going on to the next areas.*

PLATE 4-5B.

STEP 2. *For this painting, there were two sections I wanted well defined – the trees and the wet sand at the edge of the water. I painted the sand next so it would keep the ocean colors from running. Dry areas of heavy paint can be a barrier to wet paint running. It was possible to paint the trees since there is nothing next to them unpainted. The wet sand color I like is royal blue and orange mixed to a purple. The trees were painted with 75% green, 5% red, and 20% brown for the forward ones and that mixture plus royal blue for the rest. The spot of beach plant near the logs was also painted with the green mixture used very wet plus the wet sand color purple, and was applied loosely and randomly with a round brush. Then white paint was scumbled over it.*

PLATE 4-5C.

STEP 3. *The people were painted next with a very small, fine brush. Then I did several mixes of brown and royal blue for the cliffs and rocks. The darkest gray was used on the rocks. The farthest back areas of the cliffs were painted with a wetter version of that gray. Then the highlighted areas were done with a very light, bluer mix. The rest was loosely brushed with a variety of blues to browns with white scumbled over where I wanted it lightened. I did not follow the photograph closely, but looked at what was happening in the painting. Once the cliffs looked good, with good dimensionality, I went on to the water. By this time the peo-ple were dry, so I did not have to be as careful of them. If they were not dry, I would have waited to do the water. To do the water, I mixed sky blue and orange so it was a love-ly ocean green; royal blue and red; the sky blue mix and royal blue and white for a light blue. With the wet paint, I streaked the sea with the ocean green, the purple, and royal blue. Over that, I scumbled a little white. For the tide line, I first painted it with the light blue mixture and then streaked white into it in the direction of the water.*

color into it can give a more exciting quality than premixing on the palette. This also gives you an opportunity to do a little scumbling and introduce brush strokes. If you have not tried mixing on the fabric, at least do it on a sample.

SUGGESTED MIXES FOR CERTAIN AREAS:

SKY

Sky blue and a very little bit of orange. Use lots of water or add white.

SAND

Lots of white, some brown and royal blue, then a touch of red and orange.

WAVES

Pearlescent white.

MEADOW

White, ocher, and leftover sand color or violet.

WET SAND

Royal blue and orange.

TREES

Green, brown, and red. Alternate, can add some royal blue also.

BEACH PLANT

Same as trees used very wet plus the wet sand color of purple.

CLIFFS

Royal blue and brown mixed two ways, one bluer and one browner, then add white to each to have two versions lighter for a total of four mixes.

OCEAN

Sky blue and orange to a lovely ocean green. Royal blue and sky blue mixed. Royal blue and white for a light blue. A total of three mixes.

CORRECTING ERRORS

All of us drop paint where we do not want it or find an area painted too dark at some time. This is not a disaster, but an opportunity for more painterly interest. If paint is where you do not want it, first scrape it up with the palette knife. Then blot it with dry paper towels. If that is not enough, you can use wet towels and scrub it off. Sometimes I put a dry layer of folded towels underneath and use really wet ones to scrub on top.

Changing the value or color of an area is much easier and really increases the richness of the painting. Use the glazing technique to paint over. Often my meadows are too dark so I use white paint to lighten them. The paints are transparent, so the color will still show through. You may have to do this several times to achieve the value you want. The opaque white or Createx™ covering white will cover even better. However, these paints have more pigment in them so they do stiffen the fabric some. Use them with care.

If you are not pleased with your painting, do not discard it. Set it aside for awhile and then hang it up where you see it during the day. You may be surprised by what is there once you are away from it. You may have been displeased because it did not do what you expected, but it may still be a good painting. Usually it needs more work. Since you are not pleased with it, you should not hesitate to make drastic changes. You can paint over anything. Often areas need color or value changes, which can be done with overpainting or glazing. This overpainting enriches the surface. The paintings I thought were not successful, but I later finished, have turned out to be my best ones. The additional painting on them actually made them better than pieces that did not require additional effort.

Once you have a painting you are pleased with, remember to heat-set. Before I wash the painting, I do the soft-edge appliqué. The stiffness of the paint helps when sewing the appliqué. If you do not want to do the appliqué, wash the painting. Now it is just like other fabrics you are accustomed to handling.

PLATES 4-6A-E.

These quilts in progress are from a four-day class I taught in Fairbanks, Alaska. Five of the students completed their paintings and some appliqué. Several began enough of the border to have a feel for how it worked. Ree`Nancarrow sent me a slide two weeks after class with her quilt complete (Plate 5-5, page 68). None of these students except Ree had ever painted before.

PLATE 4-6A (BELOW LEFT).
DWARF DOGWOOD, 28" x 30½", Ree Nancarrow, Denali Park, Alaska, 1994.

PLATE 4-6B (BELOW RIGHT).
BIRDHOUSE IN THE FLOWERS, 18" x 22", Martha Wiedmaier, Fairbanks, Alaska, 1994.

PLATE 4-6D (ABOVE).
PICKING BLUEBERRIES, 17" x 19", Gail Flodin, Fairbanks, Alaska, 1994.

PLATE 4-6E (ABOVE).
GARDEN WITH CHAIRS, 27" x 30", Trish DeLong, Fairbanks, Alaska, 1994.

PLATE 4-6C (ABOVE). *BLUEBELL DREAM HOUSE, 36" x 30", Michel Landerman, Fairbanks, Alaska, 1994.*

Chapter 5

Soft-edge Machine Appliqué

With soft-edge machine appliqué, each piece is sewn down, either near the raw edges or repeatedly over the whole piece, with just a tiny straight stitch. When the work is washed in a washing machine, the loose edges fray, but the work stays firmly in place. The frayed edge gives a soft look to the appliqué and allows for a blending of colors not possible with the typical satin-stitched edge of machine appliqué. It is quite flexible and does not change the hand of the fabric very much, so the finished quilt has the soft, flatter look of a traditional quilt.

Combined with fabric painting, this technique gives a lovely effect because the soft edge blends well with the painting. For the sample quilt, the logs on the beach were appliquéd with this method. Since there is no hard line, they become a part of the painting. The same method of appliqué can be used without a painting as a background.

The appeal of the soft-edge machine appliqué is both with the speed of construction and without a thick line of satin stitch around the piece. It can also be done on sewing machines which do not have a zigzag stitch.

There are many applications for this type of appliqué. It works very well in wall hangings, but can be used in bed quilts and clothing, even chil-dren's clothing, and just about anything else you can sew, since it is quite strong.

MATERIALS:

Photograph or slide – your favorite landscape or another piece you wish to appliqué. Use the same photo you painted if you are embellishing that piece. If you are starting a new piece, enlarge the photograph by tracing the basic forms and then enlarging the tracing on a copy machine. For more detailed information review the drawing instructions in Chapter 2. If you have a painting to work on, use it.

SEWING MACHINE

Zigzag capability is optional, but better. Gather extra needles and your instruction book for the machine.

DARNING FOOT

This foot is for machine embroidery or darning and is available for most machines. If you cannot find one, there are spring needles available.

OPEN-TOE PRESSER FOOT

This foot is good for straight lines. (Also great if you machine quilt.) Some catalogs call it an appliqué foot.

THREAD

Different colors of thread are fun to work with so have many. Use the best quality thread you can buy. Wrapped core thread frays when used with this technique.

GLUE STICK

Use one that will wash out of fabric, not the type that goes on purple.

TRACING PAPER

Four or five sheets 8" x 10", or whatever you have on hand.

TRANSPARENT TAPE

If you need to tape several pieces of tracing paper together to cover the whole area to be appliquéd.

SCRAP PAPER

PENCIL

Soft No. 2, so it will mark on fabric.

SCISSORS

Very sharp with a fine point, such as embroidery scissors.

BASIC SEWING SUPPLIES

Scissors, pins, thimble, etc.

FABRIC

• Use your painting or a backing fabric the color of your largest area, for example light blue if you have a large area of sky.

• Many very small pieces of different colors and prints for the appliqué.

OPTIONAL

A machine embroidery hoop, freezer paper, or other stabilizer. None of these are necessary if you are using a painted background.

PREPARATION

To prepare for this technique, you do not have to gather many unusual materials. Most will already be in a typical quilter's studio. There are two sewing machine presser feet that are almost necessary to have. The darning foot is the more important and newer machines come equipped with them. If buying a darning foot and the sales person does not know what it is, explain that it is for machine embroidery. If your machine has a darning foot, it probably looks very odd to you. They all look different, but work on the same principle. There is a spring that will have a means of attaching on top of the screw for the needle. When the needle is up the foot is up; when it is down the foot is down.

If you cannot find a darning foot for your machine, there is an attachment to the needle called a spring needle. It works well on most machines. The spring comes already around a needle so you can easily see how it functions. Just put the needle in as usual and start to sew. This works almost as well as a darning foot and is easy to use. Be careful using a spring needle to keep your fingers away from the needle. It does not give the protection that a darning foot gives.

All darning feet work on the same principle. When the needle is up the foot is up, so you can move your work freely. When the needle is down the foot is down, so a good stitch is made. If you cannot move freely with the needle up, either the foot is not attached correctly or you have the wrong foot. Check your instruction manual for correct installation. The feet usually attach normally, but have an arm that goes over the screw for the needle insertion.

The other foot that is very useful for appliqué and for machine quilting, is an open-toe presser foot. Most machines do not come with this foot. It makes it easier to see the needle, but still guides the fabric with the feed dogs. The appliqué foot made for most machines does not let you see the needle as well as this open-toe foot. Most of my students who try the open-toe foot are delighted with it. If you intend to machine quilt, it really is very helpful.

PATTERNS

If you cannot see your pencil lines for placement of the appliqué (the paint may have covered them) or you do not want to draw in pencil on the fabric, you can make a guide for placing the appliqués. To make a pattern as a guide, lay a large

PLATE 5-1.
To make a placement guide for your appliqué, trace the lines on tracing paper and pin it in place. You can slip the glued fabric under the guide and use it to position the fabric.

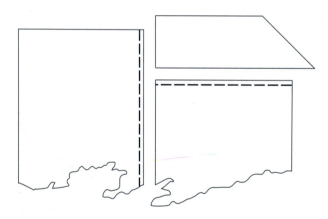

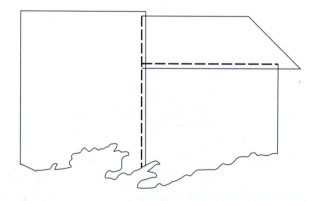

FIGURE 5-1.
Overlap diagram. The front of the building is lighter, so the side will paste over the front. The front must have ⅛" extra fabric for this overlap.

sheet of tracing paper over the area to be appliquéd or tape several small pieces together until it covers the area. You only need the tracing paper where the appliqué work is to be done, not over the whole quilt. It may be easier to divide it into sections, but have large areas grouped together. Trace an outline of all the shapes to be appliquéd onto this sheet. Set this guide aside and make the cutting patterns.

Each individual piece should be drawn on paper. I use tracing paper, but any paper that you can see through to draw the shapes will work. Trace around each piece. Think about where the pieces will overlap.

It is necessary to overlap where pieces join. The piece on top is cut to the correct shape, and the one underneath has a ⅛" edge left to fit under the top piece. This strengthens the join and keeps the backing from showing through. In hand appliqué the principle is the same. Draw onto the underneath piece an area for the lapping of ⅛". Put a notation on the pattern, perhaps x's, so you know this is to go underneath.

If possible, it is best to put dark fabrics over light so a shadow from the darker fabric will not show through light fabrics, especially solids. Check as you are working to see if the light fabric shows a shadow from the dark. Sometimes this can be used as a third color.

In order to eliminate the shadow when you must use the light fabric over the darker, a second layer of fabric can be placed under the light fabric. Either use the same fabric or a white muslin dense enough to keep the shadow edge from showing.

CUTTING

For the appliqué pieces, grain lines are secondary to the placement on the print. The pieces are all backed by the backing fabric so crazy grain lines will not affect the finished quilt. Whenever the print's pattern is not of consideration, matching the grain to the ground fabric may be a nice finishing touch, but is not necessary.

Place the paper pattern so the portion of the

fabric print is positioned as you want the piece. Pin it inside the cut line so it will not move while you work. Cut just outside the penciled line if you are being very precise with the pattern. This allows for fraying so the piece remains the size planned. Remember to follow your notations so you leave the flap for any overlapping.

FRAYING

Sometimes the perfect fabric in color and texture for your appliqué is one that frays badly. Often these are rayon or part rayon. You have several choices: you can find another fabric (really the best choice) or you can use one of the products available to prevent fraying. The disadvantage of these products is that they affect the softness or hand of the fabric, making it noticeably stiffer. Before using any product on a fabric, I do a sample pretest and wash it in the machine. If you decide to use your frayable fabric, here are five possible things to do.

- Double sew. Sew around each piece twice putting the second row of stitching just inside the first.
- Use glue. There are permanent glues at fabric stores that do not wash out, but are washable. These stiffen the most, but are very permanent.
- Use Fray check™. Carefully put a very small bead of this product on the cut edge. If you apply too much it may discolor the fabric. A test piece is recommended. This will stiffen the edge, but the body of the fabric will remain soft.
- Add iron-on interfacing. These products stiffen the most when new. The edge does not fray and will not become a soft transition, but stays as a crisp cut line. When I was making clothing, I found that iron-on interfacing separated from the fabric after several washings, so it is not very permanent.
- Place edges under neighbors. Another way to handle a problem fabric is to place its

edges underneath the pieces next to it or where satin-stitch detailing on the edges is appropriate. If you plan ahead, all the problem fabric edges may be covered this way.

Sometimes I do two of these techniques on the same piece. My MONTEREY (Plate 5-3, page 66) quilt has a brown building on it, that gave me trouble. It was applied with iron-on interfacing and double sewn. It was also quilted on the sewing line, so it was actually sewn down three times.

You almost have to try a fabric to find out how it will work, but a rule of thumb is the tighter the weave the better the fabric for this technique. This includes most of the cottons typically used for piecing. You have to select fabrics based on your experience with your collection. Some designs will benefit from loose, frayed edges and only the artist can decide if this is desired. If you want an unusual effect like very loose frayed edges and are unsure of your fabric choice, make a sample piece first.

PLATE 5-2.
Cut the pattern just outside the line to leave a little extra fabric for the fraying when it is washed.

PLATE 5-3. *MONTEREY, 58" x 58", Vicki L. Johnson, Soquel, California, © 1987. Collection of the Valley Oak Dental Group, Manteca, California. Photo by George R. Young. The buildings and the kelp are all done with soft-edge machine appliqué on this quilt. The aquarium and Stanford's marine research center are on the top with the kelp forests of Monterey Bay underneath. A harbor seal swims through the kelp. When I washed the completed top with the brown building on it, the building frayed up to the windows. I had to completely redo it, so the second time I used double sewing and iron-on interfacing.*

GLUING

If your painting or backing fabric needs ironing, it is a good idea to do so before beginning to glue the appliqué pieces onto the backing. If there are any fabrics to which you need to do extra work because they may fray, do so before you paste them down. Have a wet sponge or paper towel handy while gluing to clean the glue off your hands.

I glue each piece down as I cut. There are often many odd-shaped pieces and they get confusing if not glued in place immediately. Since I glue as I cut, the underneath pieces are applied first.

For one small quilt with a lot of appliqué, I may use three or more small glue sticks, so buy enough when you shop. Boxes of 20 can be purchased inexpensively at places like discount stores. They keep well and are useful for glueing other things. You may have to hide them from the family. It is better to have too many inexpensive glue sticks than to run out in the middle of a work session. Time to work is often hard to organize and inspiration cannot be put on a schedule. Have all supplies, and plenty of them, ready when you work.

The process of cutting and gluing can be slow because of looking at the work and making changes, but it should not be rushed. This is the most important and difficult part of the creation of your quilt.

It is self-defeating to under glue. The pieces must be held down very, very well for the sewing to go smoothly. Over gluing is no problem, because the piece will be washed and any excess glue will be removed. The glue you use must wash out of the fabric for this technique to be effective. If a glue says it is washable, it does not mean it will wash out. The fabric should return to its normal soft hand. Stay away from the glue sticks that start purple and dry clear. They have the same ink in them as the marking pens that become invisible. Some textile conservationists are reporting serious problems with these products.

Once I ran out of glue sticks and used liquid white glue that I knew would wash out. It was very messy. The pieces slid around and I had glue all over me and the backing fabric. Once it did dry, many pieces had not stuck, because the appliqué fabric had absorbed most of the glue. That was an unsuccessful experiment you do not need to repeat. The glue in the sticks is thicker and bonds to both fabrics.

When putting the glue onto the appliqué piece, apply it with the grain lines. This will help it retain its shape. Large pieces of odd shapes can really stretch. A fresh glue stick may help because the glue will be soft and not pull as much on the fabric. Work on a piece of scrap paper so you do not get glue everywhere. Cover the piece thoroughly, especially the edges. When placing it, you can restretch

PLATE 5-4.
Long, sturdy quilter's pins are great for handling the pieces with glue on them.

it once it is on the backing fabric, but not pressed down. Take two pins and repull it correctly by using the bias. Pins are handy to maneuver the glue-covered piece, especially small ones. I use extra long pins as tools to put the appliqué in place.

When working with very small pieces I have found it better to glue the backing fabric and then attach the piece. The small pieces fray at the edges if you try to apply the glue to them.

Keeping opened, but tightly recapped, glue sticks in the refrigerator may help prevent them from drying out if you use them infrequently. Glue sticks are available in larger one-ounce sizes, which are useful for the larger pieces. The smaller 26-

ounce size is the most versatile and is easier to find. I buy about 20 small ones for each large one. The smaller one is easiest to handle even with large pieces.

Pieces can be glued to the backing as you cut or later after all are cut. I like to glue as I cut for two reasons. Making a commitment in my choices keeps me from too many changes. It is better to have an overall look at what you have done before deciding one or more pieces do not work in the fabric chosen. This is best seen as a whole and looked at from a distance. Pieces that seem a little odd may be just the spark the work needs. Pin the work to a wall and look at it from 10 feet back. Look at it

PLATE 5-5. *DWARF DOGWOOD, 28" x 30½", Ree Nancarrow, Denali Park, Alaska, 1994. Photo by Ree Nancarrow. The stripes and plaids in Ree's quilt are a wonderful addition. They are an example of odd fabrics being the perfect choice. Up close you might think them too strong in this leafy painting, but they make the quilt.*

from different distances; live with it a few days. You will find yourself cutting and pinning up other choices and then looking again. The original commitment is easy to change. The glued fabric will peel off and a new one can replace it. Or you can just glue on top. My second reason for gluing as I cut is probably quite apparent now. Loose pieces would be hard to keep in place while the piece is hanging for viewing.

It is easier to sew on dried glue because wet glue gums up the needle. I also worry about it getting into the bobbin area. When I am in a hurry, I sometimes iron the glue dry. When doing this, scorching the fabric can be a problem, so I have found the nonstick press sheet I use for ironing paint works well.

PEELING

If you decide to remove a glued piece it peels off easily. Pieces with dried glue can be easier to remove than freshly glued ones. The glue helps stiffen the piece and keeps the edge from raveling.

Gently pull up the edges, then pull with the grain of the backing fabric. Work from the edges to the center. Large pieces are the most difficult, and the longer the glue has had to dry, the harder it will be to remove the piece. But, really fresh glue that has not dried at all pulls like taffy at the fabric backing. Remember to ease up the edges of other pieces that overlap the one being removed. When tearing up a large piece that has other edges overlapping it, try using the large piece to lift the edge and then pull it away from the edge. This can keep the overlapping edge from raveling. Sometimes scissor points or a pin will help. Do not let all this make you hesitate to remove any pieces you do not want because they do pull off readily.

Replace the piece removed and then reglue the overlap edges. You can place scrap paper against the overlap and fold the fabric edge back onto the paper. Then rub the glue stick over the edge, allowing the paper to take the overflow.

PREPARING FOR SEWING

Next is the sewing. Try to sew in from the edge of every piece about 3/32". This is a hard measurement to become accustomed to. Look at a ruler to familiarize yourself with the distance. Do not sew too close to the edge. When the work is washed the edges will softly ravel, so you must leave some fabric for this. However, do not sew too far from the edge either or there will be too much fabric not sewn down and it will curl. I put the edge of the work to the right while I sew, as I find it easier to see this distance.

Careful handling of the work is necessary while sewing the glued-down pieces. Since the pieces are stiffened with glue, they can lift off easily. Keeping the backing fabric flat will prevent this. Larger quilts require more careful handling because they often bend or fold while you are working on them. The smallest pieces on the quilt tend to pop off the easiest. To help with the handling, stitch the pieces near the edges of the backing fabric first. While stitching these outer areas, stitch down the smaller pieces first.

PLATE 5-6.
Use a paper against the edge for reglueing overlap. This method can also be used to glue small pieces, such as those used in broderie perse updated, without moving the pieces from their position. Put a piece of scrap paper over half of the appliqué piece. Then fold the exposed half over the paper and spread the glue. Press the glued portion down and repeat on the other half.

If you are appliquéing glued pieces to a painting, it should be quite stiff compared to regular fabric and you should be able to handle it easily, without resorting to a hoop or backing. If you are working on an unpainted background or one that seems too soft when you start to stitch, a hoop or backing may help. For small areas of appliqué a hoop is fine as you can center the appliqué in the hoop. If the glued appliqué is caught under the hoop, it may cause it to lift up, so care is needed. For larger work, backings such as paper or products that tear off from the stitching can help. Ironing the backing to freezer paper is another possibility. If you use paper, it has to be pulled away from the stitching when you are finished. This can be quite tedious and you may need tweezers to remove it. Some products dissolve when sprayed with water, which helps with removal. If you intend to wash the piece as I do once the appliqué is finished, spray starch can be used as a stabilizer. Several light coats with ironing between coats works best. With a painted background I have never needed to use a hoop or paper.

When selecting thread for use in the sewing machine, you should use the best quality available. Cotton-wrapped thread with a polyester core does not work well when stitching through many layers. Especially with free-motion work the wrapped thread frays at the needle, so I do not use it. Either polyester thread or cotton thread works, but the cotton will fray at the needle before the polyester. Purists use all cotton. They feel the polyester threads will cut the fabric before it breaks because it is stronger than the cotton of the fabric. I have quilts I quilted with polyester thread 20 years ago, that have had hard use. The thread broke first. In some areas the fabric is worn out and the stitching has held. In my experience, thread cutting the fabric is not a problem. Use cotton or polyester, whichever you prefer. If you are making a wall quilt, the effect of the thread is more important than the strength. Polyester has a bit more sheen than cotton. Recently, I acquired silk thread, which shines even more, and I have been having fun using it. There are many lovely shiny colors and metallics that can be exciting to use.

For the soft-edge work, I usually match the color of the appliqué fabric as best I can. When you want the thread to blend, the value is more important than the hue. All the grays I can find are in my thread collection. A gray tone nearest the value of the fabric will blend well. I use a medium gray for much of the appliqué and the quilting, too.

Another interesting effect is to use the stitched line to add color and interest. Think of it as a drawn line around the piece. Would that be interesting in a color different from the fabric? Would a blue thread enhance and pull out the blue in the print? Ask yourself these types of questions when deciding the thread color.

SEWING

There are two methods you need to know to do the sewing – straight stitching and free-motion stitching. With the straight lines, an open-toe presser foot works best. You can use one of the regular feet of your machine, but this one really lets you see the needle. Gauging the distance from the edge is very hard if you cannot see the needle well. With the curved lines, a darning foot works best. It lets you move freely so even tight curves are easy.

If you have done machine quilting before, your open-toe presser foot may have a scratched line from the needle. This sometimes happens when you move too fast and the needle bends enough to hit the foot. This scratch can be useful in positioning the work for the very accurate stitching we will be doing. When I changed machines and feet, I realized how helpful this scratch was, so I purposely scratched my new foot. Put the foot on the machine and lower the needle. With a strong pin or other pointed metal object, using the needle as a guide by lining up on it, scratch a small line on the foot. Once you have it marked you can remove the foot and make the scratch deeper until it is easy to see. This line is also useful for machine quilting.

Sometimes it is easier to watch the thread line you are forming than the needle. It is hard to look at the moving needle. Some machines require the thread in the bobbin match the top thread in weight or type. If you are skipping stitches, this is the first thing to check.

When you first begin to do this type of sewing it is especially important to take breaks. Very accurate stitching is necessary, so at first you will probably become tense. Even now I find it necessary to break after an hour of sewing to rest my eyes and loosen my shoulders.

STRAIGHT STITCH SEWING

Set your machine for regular straight stitch sewing, but select a very short stitch length. This is about 14 stitches to the inch or on some machines a number 1. You want a stitch as short as possible, but do not want thread to build up in ridges. The tighter stitch enables you to stitch closer to the edge so the shape of the piece remains accurate in size.

Sew all the way around each piece. To start, select a spot where either the piece joins another or where you plan to do zigzag detail. Another spot to start is on the edge that will later be covered by binding or seams. If none of these is possible, begin where two lines of stitching will show the least. Sew all the way around the piece and return to the starting stitches. Then cross over the starting stitches with at least three stitches to lock the thread (Figure 5-2). If you start where you cannot return to cross over the stitches, do a couple of back stitches to secure the thread. A long pin is handy to hold in place any points that pop up while sewing.

When you have two pieces joining, sew in the ditch on the bottom piece. When sewing the other piece in the top position, sew the ³⁄₃₂" away from the join edge as this will be a fabric edge. By doing this, you are sewing all the pieces down completely and sewing doubly at the join (Figure 5-3). If you are having difficulty seeing that all the pieces have been stitched down, run your finger around them. It will be easy to feel the stitches.

PLATE 5-7.
Scratching a line on the open-toe presser foot at the center can help you judge where you are stitching.

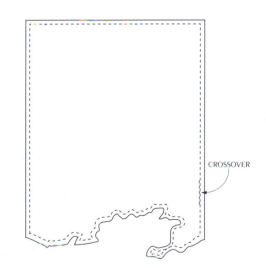

CROSSOVER

FIGURE 5-2.
Diagram for starts and stops. Sew all the way around each shape and cross over three stitches.

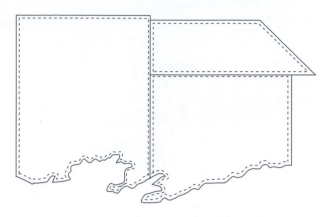

FIGURE 5-3.

Sewing diagram for joins. Sew around each piece. Where pieces join there will be two lines of stitching: one on the top piece 3/32" from the edge and one on the lower piece in the ditch.

PLATE 5-8.

Hold your hands in a hoop position while doing free-motion stitching.

PLATE 5-9.

This is an alternate position for your fingers while doing free-motion stitching.

FREE-MOTION SEWING

Free-motion sewing is just like machine embroidery, and those of you who have done machine embroidery will know the basic technique. Free-motion quilting uses the same technique, so time spent now learning to use the darning foot properly will also be helpful when you try to do machine quilting.

Set up your machine as for darning and attach the darning foot or spring needle. Lower the feed dogs, if you can. If your machine does not allow you to lower them, do not be concerned. I have used a machine successfully which could not do this. If the moving feed dogs bother you, reduce your stitch length to as close to 0 as you can. Or tape a piece of very thin cardboard over the feed dogs. If you have never used a darning foot, a practice piece is very important.

You will determine the stitch length. The feed dogs are no longer feeding the fabric. Find the point where the machine runs smoothly and you are in control. Some people run the machine very fast and others very slow. Do whatever gives you the most control. With the darning foot, you can move in any direction since the presser foot is no longer holding the fabric in place. When the needle is up the foot is up, so you can move freely.

You must remember to lower the presser foot lever just as you normally do. The stitches do not form properly if it is not lowered. Everyone forgets once in awhile. Train yourself to check this first if your stitches begin to look odd or skip.

Hold your hands on each side of the work with fingers spread (Plate 5-8). This forms a hoop and gives you the control to move where you wish.

Some machines require you to hold the thread for the first stitches. Either take one stitch and with the top thread pull the bobbin thread up or turn the flywheel so one stitch is taken and pull up the bobbin thread. Then you can hold both from the top. Take the first several stitches and once the thread is firmly locked in the fabric, clip the threads you were holding. Try sewing your name several times and you will begin to have a feel for free-motion work.

Clip threads as best as you can while you sew. Then they won't get caught in the foot or especially the bobbin. You can move from one area to the next without clipping if the threads stay taut.

Again you will be stitching 3/32" from the edge, just as you did with straight stitching. Try to move so your stitch length is the same as the straight stitching sample of very close stitching. If you run your finger over the stitched line, it should feel all on the same level with no areas of thread built up. If thread builds up you are moving too slowly. Do not worry about uneven stitches. They will still hold and should not show if you matched the thread to the appliqué fabric. With practice, you will gain control of the stitch length so it is even.

All the same methods of starting, stopping, and sewing joins are the same as described with straight stitching.

DETAILS

For added interest, details can be embroidered onto the appliqué as I did on the porches in my Mendocino quilts. They are satin stitched on after all pieces have been sewn down. Embroidery does

hold the edge firmly, but I do not use it as an attaching method. All the satin stitching is for adding detail. Other types of embroidery could also be used as long as they are washable.

To do the satin stitch, reduce your machine's top tension by half of the normal tension setting. For example, if you sew with a top tension of 5, use 2.5 to do the satin stitch. This will make a smoother laying stitch with the top thread pulled to the back and no bobbin thread on the top. Do a test sample checking the settings until you have a smooth stitch.

WASHING AND CLIPPING

Once the sewing is completed, the entire piece goes into the washing machine. This removes excess paint stiffness and frays the edges of the appliqué. Wash the piece as you plan to wash the finished quilt. I now wash everything in Orvus®. Putting the piece in the dryer is the step that frays the appliqué edge.

Be prepared for dismay when you first remove your piece from the dryer. I have never pulled one out and not felt I had ruined it. But, after you have clipped all of the frayed ends you do not want, the

PLATE 5-10.
Here I have jumped from one area to another. As long as the thread stays taut and there are not too many threads to catch on the presser foot, you can continue stitching.

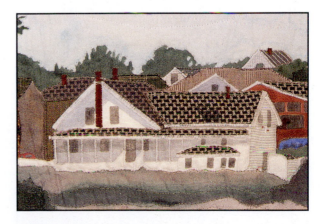

PLATE 5-11.
MENDOCINO SPRING, Vicki L. Johnson. Detail of Plate 8-6, page 104. On these Mendocino houses you can see the satin-stitch details. The stitching is done only as an embroidered detail.

PLATE 5-12.
In this detailed photograph of BEACHWALKERS you can see all the loose frayed threads from washing.

PLATE 5-13.
BEACHWALKERS with the appliqué finished.

real work will emerge.

Clip only the long loose ends. If you clip too close to the stitching, the next time you wash the piece, the edges will fray again.

You do not have to clip the rough edges if a softer effect is better. These loose threads are not as permanent as the sewn down ones, but for a wall hanging they could stay.

Even if you do not clip, you must very carefully go over every edge. Handle them and run your fingers over them. Whenever you find a loose edge, put in a pin. Do not be surprised if the top seems covered with pins. It really is not as many as it may seem. Re-sew wherever you have pinned. Usually, this can be done in a surprisingly short time. Now you can be sure the edges will all stay sewn down. If you quilt on the appliqué, you can add a second sewing of the edges for extra assurance.

VARIATIONS

With the soft-edge appliqué technique, there are other possibilities. An area can be textured by using many very small pieces. These can even be toned to shade a space. Randomly glue many small pieces into a shape. Sew randomly or around each piece. If the pieces are very small, random stitching is best as it can be very tedious to go around each piece. Diane Williams used this technique to make a spray of autumn leaves framing HALF-DOME AUTUMN, by sewing loosely around each piece (Plate 5-14).

Reverse appliqué can also be done effectively with this technique. Place several layers of different colored fabrics on top of each other. Sew the top shape and then cut away the inside of that shape through the first fabric. Continue sewing and cutting until the last fabric is showing.

BRODERIE PERSE UPDATED

Another interesting variation updates broderie perse. Detailed designs, such as printed roses, can be added to your quilt by cutting them out of commercial fabrics. Paste them down and then sew around them with the darning foot using tiny stitches. If you are doing a landscape, observe carefully so the smaller items are farthest away and the larger ones are in the foreground. This will keep things in perspective. Selecting elements from fabric with a background which blends with your background is best. In my ROSE BARN (Plate 5-16) the roses in the foreground came from a black background. That works because shadows would be around the foliage and because the painting is at dusk. In a daytime version, lighter backgrounds would be better, with meadow or yellow colors being the best.

When cutting the small pieces, select groups, three or four roses with their leaves. Then cut a distance of two or three threads away from the image. It helps to use very sharp scissors and to hold the scissors still while feeding the fabric into them.

When sewing the larger pieces in place, it is best to change the colors of thread so you emphasize the form of the item – like pink on the rose and green on the leaves. With the very small ones, there are two choices. They can be sewn around carefully so each piece is held, or they can be freely sewn like doodling all over them with a colored line of

PLATE 5-14. *HALF-DOME AUTUMN, 22" x 28", Diane Williams, Twain Harte, California, 1989. Diane used a texturing technique to float aspen leaves across the top of her quilt. Each leaf has been sewn down separately, but she could have randomly sewn them.*

PLATE 5-15.
These four rose prints were used to do the roses on my ROSE BARN (Plate 5-16). Made by the same manufacturer, they blended well and gave me a wide range of sizes.

thread. When washed the loose sewing will have more fraying, but will still be strong. For a very textural area, that could be quite exciting.

In my small quilt SPRING AT THE FARM (Plate 5-17), I used very small prints and had many details to sew around. If you doubt your ability to sew around so many details, this would be a good time to use iron-on interfacing, but it does stiffen the fabric quite a bit. After sewing clothes with iron-on interfacing and washing them I have found

PLATE 5-16. *ROSE BARN, 36" x 36", Vicki L. Johnson, Soquel, California © 1993. Private collection. This rose-covered building quietly sits along the Mendocino coast north of town. Until I thought of cutting the roses out of fabric, doing this scene eluded me.*

it not to be permanent. However, you will not be washing a wall hanging frequently, so that is not as much of a concern. A few small details stiffened with interfacing will not affect the look of the quilt if you use it selectively. If you do decide to use iron-on interfacing, select the lightest weight you can find.

With the variety of prints available today, updated broderie perse offers many possibilities. If you want to try it, start collecting fabric. The more choices you have, especially in different sizes, the better your quilt will be. A print with several sizes of roses, from less than one inch up to three or four inches, is a great find for this technique.

Once the appliqué step is finished, you are ready to add whatever borders or other treatments you wish. Some quilts, such as my underwater ones, are complete appliqué tops at this stage and can be quilted.

PLATE 5-17. *SPRING AT THE FARM, 24" x 36", Vicki L. Johnson, Soquel, California, © 1995. Photo: Charley Lynch. Using flowers from different fabrics works well if you keep sizes and color in mind. By having very small roses at the back and building to larger flowers, I created a feeling of distance. Softer colors work best in the background with brighter flowers in the foreground.*

PLATE 5-18. *SEALS AND GARIBALDIS IN THE KELP, 48" x 48",*
Vicki L. Johnson, Soquel, California, © 1992. Photo by George R. Young. Kelp is
particularly wonderful done in soft-edge machine appliqué since it really does have a
serrated edge which the frayed fabric suggests.

Chapter 6

Adding Pieced Borders

When you have completed your painting, you need to decide on the pieced border treatments. This can be as simple or complex as you wish to make it. For my example, I am adding two rows of squares and a stripped border. The following chapter gives directions for my border. Making your own additions will personalize your quilt.

MATERIALS:

BORDER FABRICS

- Precut 3½" squares in the colors you plan for your piece. Half should be solids. Remember the sky is very light.
- A few plaids to cut 1" strips for the tucked border.
- Many 1" wide strips of fabric 4" or longer in your colors, for the strip-pieced border.
- A piece of muslin 4" x the width of your painting plus 1". The muslin is a backing fabric.

FLANNEL

A white piece bigger than your planned work – at least 30" x 36". Hang this piece on the wall and pin pieces of border fabric to it so you can stand back from the work and view it. If you cannot hang it on the wall, back the flannel with cardboard so you can prop it against a wall or furniture.

ROTARY CUTTER, MAT, AND RULER
SEWING MACHINE
NORMAL SEWING TOOLS FOR PIECING

TRIMMING

Once the appliqué is washed and clipped, it is ready for the border treatments. Iron it again, and prepare to trim it to size. The rotary cutter is the best tool for this. Carpenters measure twice and cut once. So should you. Trimming is critical. A mistake here is hard to adjust.

Before you trim, you should have decided on a module for the rest of the quilt. A module is a component size that you multiply to create the overall size of your piece. I use a three-inch module, so our sample quilt is made with that module. (For a diagram of modules, see Figure 4-2, page 53). The suggested painting size, based on three-inch modules, was 12" x 15". You must add seam allowances, so trim 12½" x 15½", if you are using the suggested sample size.

There are other ways to arrange a border. Before you make a decision, you may want to look at the examples in the photographs. Many of my students chose to do very creative things with their borders. In the directions, I will continue using the suggested size as an example.

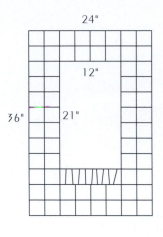

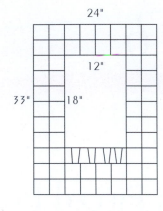

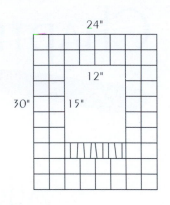

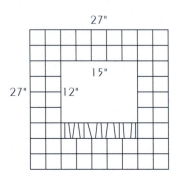

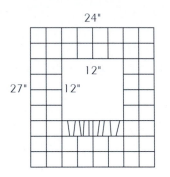

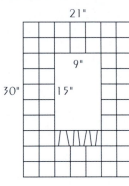

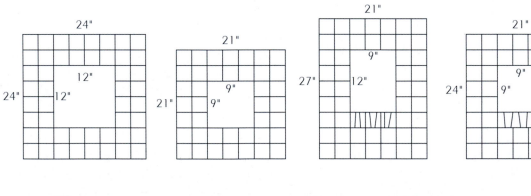

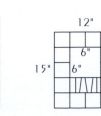

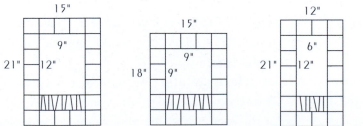

FIGURE 6-1.

Good sizes for small quilts: based on 3" module size I use most.

Because of changes in your painting, you may choose to make a different size or to crop the painting differently. This happens to me, too. Just make sure the size is in multiples of three inches, or your chosen module, plus seams. Measure the top to see where you want to trim it and lightly pencil crop marks on the part you expect to remove.

Place the ironed painting on the cutting mat squared up with the lines. The most important line to have correct is the horizontal horizon line. Even in nature the ocean is perfectly level. If this element is not in your work, the next one to have straight would be buildings or strong verticals – people standing, flagpoles, animals, straight fences. The viewer expects these things to be straight vertically and will notice immediately if they are not. If you have several of these elements and need to choose, the most prominent one needs to be correct.

Use your clear cutting ruler and place it over the element you want straight. Line it up with the proposed cutting line. On small quilts, you can usually line up the edge parallel to and nearest that element at the same time. If the edge is also the edge of the fabric, or very near to it, go ahead and cut this side. A large square ruler, 12" x 12", is very helpful. You may need to place another ruler or triangle against your ruler to both reach the edge and line up on the element.

Turn the matt, with the quilt top on it, so you can cut comfortably. Put the ruler where you expect

PLATE 6-1. *THE BURNING HUT, 28" x 28", Jill Le Croissette, Carlsbad, California, 1991. Private collection. Photo by Dennis Le Croissette. Jill wanted something different as a subject for her painting and selected a photo of fire for its subject and color. This unusual subject of a burning hut has special meaning for Jill as it is a memory of Australia for her. She grew up in Sydney where bush fires were prevalent. Any subject that has meaning for you, is a good choice for your painting. The vertical lines of the border piecing add to a feeling of flames.*

FIGURE 6-2 (STEPS 1-7).
Construction Steps – once painting is finished.

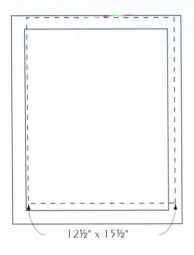

12½" x 15½"

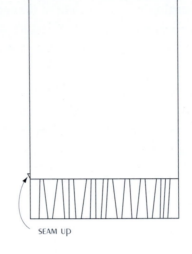

SEAM UP

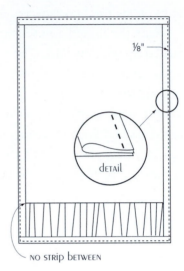

⅛"

detail

NO STRIP BETWEEN

STEP 1.
Example shows how you may crop differently than originally planned. Trim size 12½" x 15½".

STEP 2.
Sew strip to painting. Seams up.

STEP 3.
With ⅛" seam attach 1" strip folded in half to painting. Edge of painting and edge of folds match.

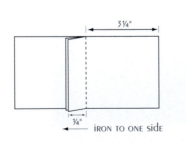
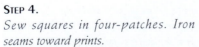

3¼"

¼"

IRON TO ONE SIDE

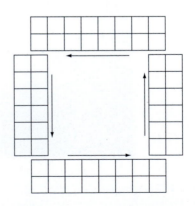

STEP 4.
Sew squares in four-patches. Iron seams toward prints.

STEP 5.
Attach side rows to the painting first. As best you can, iron seams in the direction of the arrows. Use a ¼" seam.

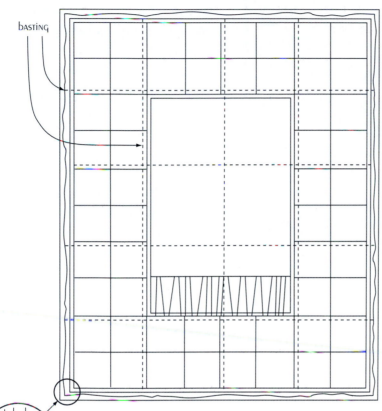

basting

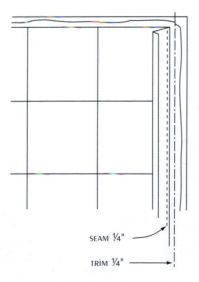

STEP 6.

Basting. Leave extra batting and backing. Baste near, not on, proposed quilting lines.

SEAM ¼"

TRIM ¼"

STEP 7.

After quilting, put on the binding. Sewing line with top edge as guide. Trim line ¼" from top edge.

PLATE 6-2. *PIGEON PT. BARNS, Vicki L. Johnson. Detail of Plate 1-3, page 11. This is a closeup of a stripped border and tucked edge.*

the edge parallel to the one you just cut, to be cut. Use another ruler or tape measure to check this measurement by measuring from the cut edge to the edge of the cutting ruler. It is important to use a tape measure as long as the side measured. If you have to do two measurements, you will make mistakes.

Your ruler should have lines perpendicular to its edge. These lines help you square the cuts perpendicular to the ones you just made. Where you expect the next side to be, lay the ruler. Use the lines to square this edge. Again, the large square ruler is helpful. Use it to make the corners square and butt the longer ruler against it, if you need length for the side you are cutting. When you are sure this is correct, cut the fabric. Otherwise, draw a pencil line and check it with a triangle or square ruler to see that it is square. Go to the parallel side, and place the ruler where you expect to cut. Measure from the pencil line and draw another pencil line on the fabric. Remeasure each edge with a tape as long as the quilt top, by checking in at least three

PLATE 6-3.
On top of a backing muslin, place two strips at an angle, right sides together. Sew with a ¼" seam allowance. Iron or finger press them open.

PLATE 6-4.
To continue the strip-pieced border, place a third strip at an angle to the first two and sew. Iron open. Continue in this manner until the backing muslin is covered.

places (top, middle, and bottom) to be sure they are parallel. Then with a triangle or square ruler, check the corners to see that they are square. If correct, trim on your pencil lines.

If you have extra fabric or are unsure of your trimming lines, do not cut until you have all four sides decided. Use very light pencil lines to indicate where you think you want to cut. Once all four sides are drawn you can return to these steps and cut. There are fabric erasers available if you need to erase some of your pencil lines.

STRIP PIECING

Under my painting, I like to put a border of strips that repeat the colors in the painting. This can reflect the cliffs in a coastal landscape or the logs on the beach. A scene with a meadow in the foreground could be an abstraction of the grasses. It could also have the feeling of geological layers of land below the surface. It will depend on the colors chosen and the painting.

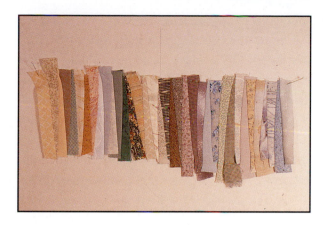

PLATE 6-6.
This is the strip-pieced border I attached to BEACH-WALKERS.

PLATE 6-7. (BELOW)
If you have made the strip-pieced border a bit longer than the painting is wide, you can try it in different positions until the colors balance well with the painting. Before you trim the strip-pieced border, sew it onto the painting. Iron the seam toward the painting. There are too many thicknesses of fabric in the border to fold.

PLATE 6-5.
To save time making the strip-pieced border, you can start in the middle and sew toward each end. Sew on each end and then iron the strips open.

If you choose to make the border of strip piecing under the painting, it is very much like crazy patchwork. Precut many different one-inch strips of your fabrics and place them beside your machine. The strips must be at least 4" long, but if longer they can be trimmed after sewing. Set the machine for normal straight-stitch sewing. If you can, put the iron and ironing board to one side of your machine, so you can reach them without standing.

In the middle of the muslin backing fabric, place a strip at an angle faceup. Place a second strip facedown on top of it. Stitch with a ¼" seam through all three layers using the edge of the strip as a guide. Fold the top strip back so it is faceup and iron the seam flat.

Place another strip of fabric facedown on one of the other strips, but at an angle. Sew this piece along its edge. Fold it back and iron it flat. You should now have three strips in place. The seams are at different angles. Continue stripping until the muslin is covered.

If you work from the middle out, you can speed the work. When you have placed four or five strips you can start working both ends. Sew a strip onto each end and then iron.

Pick up the fabrics at random for a greater variation. The stripping looks better if it is not too planned. Remember to put in an occasional solid fabric. I hang my painting above my sewing machine so I can look at it for color choices while working.

Once the muslin is covered, trim it to 3½" in height. Do not trim the ends. Sew it onto the bottom of the painting and iron the seams toward the painting. Lay the piece on your cutting mat. Using the edge of the painting as a guide, trim off the extra strip piecing to the same width as the painting.

SQUARES

For my smaller quilts, I like to create a border of squares around the painting. This frames the work and enhances the colors. I continue the landscape into the border of squares with the color and value of the fabrics I use. Three-inch squares are my module choice to work with, but any size will work. Other piecing could be used, but could become more of a definite frame. For instance, blocks of particular quilt patterns would probably frame the scene and not continue it. Sometimes students have used triangles to reflect mountains in their painting and this is very effective. Piecing used in a manner to repeat forms in the scene would be best.

It is important to plan the square border vertically so you can step back and look at the piece. If you do not have a pin board, hang a piece of flannel larger than the proposed quilt on a wall or other vertical surface. If you cannot hang it, back it with foam-core board or cardboard so you can prop it up. Many quilters have a wall where they have hung a piece of wallboard. Some cover this wallboard with white flannel or fleece so the pieces stick without pins. This allows them to look at the quilt vertically.

Pin the painting and strip-pieced border onto the pinup wall or flannel. Some quilters just press pieces to flannel and they will stay. This works for me for working periods, but I pin the pieces if I am leaving the work overnight or longer so breezes created by dog tails or people walking past will not disturb the pieces.

Alternate the printed squares with solid ones in a four-patch arrangement. The solid color gives a resting area to the busyness of the prints. Look at the painting and continue the values and colors out into the border. Consider the planes of the landscape when studying the painting.

Unlike typical patchwork, you do not contrast the colors and values next to each other. If a brown cliff is at the left edge of the painting, use two brown prints and two brown solids together with the same value and tones as the painting. Look at the color photos for examples of this. The colors in the painting can be enhanced depending on the particular fabrics used. If the brown cliffs have dark blue shadows, a dark blue fabric or one with blue in the brown print can enrich the blues in the painting.

PLATE 6-8. *HERMOSA BEACH PIER, 23" x 21¾", Lois Pio, Hermosa Beach, California, © 1994. Photo by Susan Einstein. Lois used her own hand-dyed fabrics to continue her painting into the first border. In some areas, she used triangles to continue the forms more than squares would. Then she chose to use a wide gray border. This makes a definite frame for the rest of the work. With her beautiful quilting in this border, the effect is quite lovely. More interest is added with shells and buttons.*

PLATE 6-9.

Usually I put all the print squares in place before I add the solids. I have many more choices in prints than solids, so I like to settle them first.

Or you can tone down a color by not using it. You will probably want to repeat many of the fabrics used in the strip-pieced border, but do not feel you must use only those fabrics.

Calicoes with small busy flower prints do not work with a landscape unless you have a garden or a flower-filled meadow. Geometric prints which are more like textures are better. Large prints cut into three-inch squares become quite abstract and often work well. The backs of fabrics can be used, too. Backs are softer and may be just what is needed.

Wait to sew all of this together, especially on larger quilts. Every piece is in relationship to the whole and can change the effect. If you sew parts together, you are making a commitment. Avoid sewing as long as you can. This keeps you flexible.

PLATE 6-10.

Before I sew any squares together I choose the tucked edge fabric. Often there are several possibilities. This tucked edge brings out the white and blue of the ocean – a possible choice, but I did not want to emphasize the water. You can see the one I selected in Plate 6-11. It brings out the pink and lavender in the quilt.

PLATE 6-11.

For the tucked edge, a one-inch fabric strip folded in half is sewn onto the painting with a ⅛" seam allowance. The sides are sewn first and then the top and bottom. Now that the tucked edge has been sewn onto BEACHWALKERS, it is ready to have the squares sewn together and attached.

TUCKED EDGE

Around the painting and the strip-pieced border, I put a plaid tucked edge. This makes a nice transition between the painting and the printed fabric. Plaids seem to work best since they have several colors in small amounts. Folded and in a small strip they become slashes of color. Select a plaid which reflects the color tones and values in your painting. Selecting a plaid edge can be an interesting experience. In one class, a student was considering three different plaids. All three worked, but each made a different part of the painting stand out. She needed to decide which part was most important to her. Stand back after you arrange the strip in position to look at the total effect.

The tucked strip can be selected before you do the three-inch square selection, but I find it is better to do it last. The squares add to the overall piece much more than the strip. The strip is easier to change to accommodate what is happening with the squares.

To construct the strip, cut a one-inch strip of plaid as long as the distance around your painting. Fold the strip in half with right sides out and iron it. Sew it onto the painting with a ⅛" seam allowance using the raw edges as a guide. By using this narrow seam allowance, you will not have stitching showing when you sew the squares to the painting. Sew the vertical sides first and trim to the length after it is sewn in place. Repeat for the horizontal sides, overlapping at the corners.

SEWING IT ALL TOGETHER

The squares are sewn together in four-patches and then in strips. Iron the seams of the four-patches toward the prints. See the appendix if you need instruction on basic patchwork construction. Connect the four-patches in rows so you have a top section and a bottom section. Each side section is then sewn together.

So the seams are all laying away from the presser foot when you sew these rows to the painting, iron them in a counter-clockwise pattern (see

PLATE 6-12.
The four rows of squares are ready to be attached to the painting.

PLATE 6-13.
Sew the squares to the work from the back of the painting. That way the tucked edge strip will be even and ¼" wide. The feed dogs will ease in any differences in the squares. First sew the side squares to the painting. This top is now complete.

Figure 6-2, page 82, step 5). Attach the sides to the painting with a ¼" seam allowance and iron with seams away from the painting. Then sew on the top and bottom row of squares in the same manner.

LABELING

Signing your quilt is very important. Unless you do, your grandchildren will not know if the quilts they inherit were made by you or someone not in the family. It will mean much more to them to know who made it. If quilts are sold, it adds to their value in all ways for the artist's name and the date made to be clearly on the quilt. Part of the reason so much of women's art – quilts – has been undervalued, is in its anonymity. The attitude seems to be, if the maker does not value it enough to sign, why should anyone else value it.

Sign your name clearly on the front, but work it into a design area. Also put it on the back with any other information you want to include. That can simply be the date made and its title or pattern. Or it can be the complete story of the quilt's creation. If you really want to tell a long story, you could make a sealable pocket on the back where you put your story written on either paper or fabric. In Chapter 3 there is a discussion of marking pens and their permanence.

Since 1978 the copyright law says a work of art is copyrighted if the maker's name, copyright symbol (©), and the date are on the work where they are easy to see. I put this basic information on the front of all my quilts. Quilts may or may not be fine art, but they are craft and copyrights do cover crafts. Putting this information on your quilts at least gives you minimal coverage; without it you have none. If you really want to protect your design, contact the copyright office in Washington, D.C. or a lawyer.[1]

Now the top for your small quilt is complete, unless you have ideas for additional embellishment. Attaching beads, buttons, or other three-dimensional objects is best done after the quilting. Iron the piece well so it lays flat in preparation for basting.

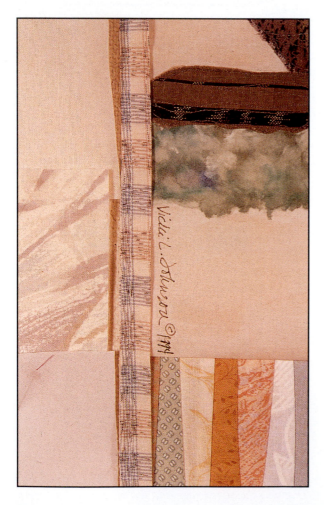

PLATE 6-14.
Do not forget to sign your work! I sign the front with a ©, name, and year. On the back I repeat that information and add the title.

[1]*Professional Quilter, Issues 39, 40, & 41, Oliver Press, 104 Bramblewood Lane, Lewisberry, PA 17339-9535*

CHAPTER 7

QUILTING PREPARATION

Once the top is complete, you need to prepare it for quilting. Press the top and hang it on your pin wall, so it does not wrinkle. Find a fabric for the backing which has a small print. Designs with strong direction, such as stripes, are difficult to use as backs. Directional prints can be used, but it is difficult to line up the top to the back with the lines of the print. If it is off a little, it looks like a mistake. Let it really go off and it looks more purposeful. A small print is more forgiving if your quilting stitches are not perfect.

Some quilters like to do back-art on their quilts. I spend my creative time on the front. Backs usually are to a wall and no one sees them. Coordinating the backing fabric to the top is a nice finishing touch that I like to do.

Do not skimp on the fabric for the back. Fabric shop flat-fold tables can supply good backing fabrics, but you must be careful in your selection. For my SUNSET SEA (Plate 11-12, page 137) and SUNSET SEA II (Plate 9-2, page 109), I spent almost $10.00 a yard for fabric, because I found the perfect print to reflect the top. After a year of work, it deserved that special print. The fabric should be the same weight as the quilt top fabrics. Too soft and the quilting lines will not puff; too heavy and the top will wear more than the back.

Cut or tear a piece of backing fabric two inches larger on each side than the top of your quilt. This leaves room for basting and any possible movement while quilting. Press the backing and pin it to the wall on top of your quilt top to check the size and to keep it flat.

BATTING

Next, select the batting. This is very important and should be done with some care. If you are experienced with machine quilting, you probably have a favorite batt. For most of my work, I have used polyester batting. It works very well and gives a nice puff to the quilt.

Recently, I tested all the batts I could acquire as samples. I wanted to see how they worked with machine quilting and how they washed. Some shrink quite a bit when they are washed. Quilters who use batts that may shrink sometimes prewash them. This is extra work and I prefer to do as little as possible. Other quilters like the old-fashioned look of a shrinking batt and wash only after quilting. This testing was very interesting. Every quilter would benefit from doing it. Get together with other quilters and exchange ten-inch squares of batting. Then make a mini quilt from each. Mark the unwashed measurements on the back with permanent pen. Wash the sample and remeasure. Record this measurement. When you have a group of samples you can see the differences in the batting and select the effect you want.

The most visable difference is between cotton and polyester batts. Cotton gives a flatter look, similar to older quilts. Polyester puffs more. Depending on the thickness of the polyester batt, you can decide how much puff you want. Thicker polyester batts are more difficult to machine quilt because the top slides more between the presser foot and the batting. The cotton batts held the top in place while it was quilted.

For my recent quilts, I have been using cotton batting. It is easy to quilt and has some puff. The finished quilt hangs better than with polyester. The look is not as flat as some quilters like, but not as puffy as the polyester batts. I like the idea of using cotton and not a synthetic, since it is a renewable resource.

Cut the batting about one inch larger on each side than your top and set it aside. If you are doing a large quilt, cut it two inches larger on each side.

BASTING

When I baste a quilt, I usually use thread in lines straight to the grain. This holds the quilt in place without stretching. Some machine quilters like to pin baste with safety pins. Done well, this seems to work fine. There are two reasons I do not use pins. Quilting around them is difficult, so you have to stop and remove the pin. More importantly, the pins are quite fat when big enough to use for basting, and would leave big holes in the painting. Painted fabric does not repair itself like regular fabric, since it has the pigment on it. For each pinhole, I might need to force the threads back in place with a pin or my fingernail and this is tedious. With a thin needle, this is not as much of a problem.

For a small quilt, place the backing face down on a table larger than the quilt. Use a table that needles or pins will not scratch. Tape the back to the table. Do not stretch it, but have it taut. Make sure the grain lines are straight. Tape the corners first and then opposite sides across the middle. Continue to work around the quilt in this manner. By taping opposite sides, you can keep the grain straight.

Place the batting on top of the backing and smooth it, but do not stretch it. Put the top, face up, onto the batting. Center it on the backing, so you have extra backing fabric all around the top. First pin the corners so the top is square and smoothed. It can be stretched a little, but too much will cause problems with the quilting. Continue to pin by doing the centers of each side first and working opposite sides in the same pattern as for taping. This will help to retain the square corners. Check with a triangle to see if you have all sides squared.

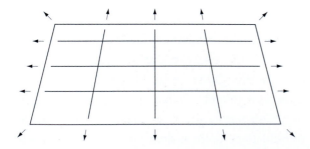

FIGURE 7-1.
Tape quilt back to table top in preparation for basting.

FIGURE 7-2.
Bury your pins in the batting when pinning for basting.

If it is not square now, it never will be later.

My first quilting teacher taught me to bury the points of the pins in the batting. This does not take much time and keeps you from scratching your hands on the pins, which is painful and often gets blood on the quilt!

Sew all layers together ¼" in from the edges with a running stitch about one inch long. You can remove the pins as you go. This sewing secures the edge and is not removed until after the first edge of binding is applied. For the rest of the basting, longer stitches can be used.

Baste the rest of the quilt with lines of stitching six inches apart both vertically and horizontally. If you have used the three-inch module, you can use the spacing in your quilt as a guide. Sew next to, but not on, the lines you plan to quilt. If you baste on the quilting lines, it will be difficult to remove the basting thread after the machine stitching is done. Basting across areas that you want to puff up sometimes leaves a flattened ridge, so try to baste close to the planned quilting lines. When you do this, the basting can be used as a marking method.

MATERIALS

White thread is best for basting. With white there is no danger the thread will leave color tracks on the quilt. Any sewing thread you have will work as long as it does not break. Thread does deteriorate if kept for a long time. If you can break it easily with your hands, it is too old.

The needle you use should be sturdy and long, but not too fat. In the painted portions where the paint is thick, the needle will leave holes. Later, you can take your fingernail or a pin and rub across the hole to force the threads back in place. This is not so necessary if the needle is thin. Long needles work best when basting, since more needle protrudes from the quilt to grab. Curved needles are great, but require practice. Buy the thinnest needles you can find of good quality.

To help grab the needle and pull it through the layers, a thimble that looks like a guitar pick can be

PLATE 7-1.
When basting, I found myself picking up the needle point with my fingernail. This broke nails, so I tried this plastic thimble turned around. It works and saves nails.

PLATE 7-2.
Curved needles make basting easier, but you must buy good quality thin ones or they leave holes in the fabric.

used. Wear it backwards over your own nail on the index finger of your left hand if you are right handed. It is used to lift the point of the needle.

BASTING LARGE QUILTS

Quilts too large for a table can be basted two ways. If you have access to several tables, you can put them together and tape the quilt across them. This will probably require sitting on the table and laying across the quilt to reach the center. The quilters in the Santa Rosa Quilt Guild did this when I was a member. Tables were available at their meeting space, so several members would work together and baste large quilts at one meeting.

I have found it is easy for me, working alone, to put a quilt in a frame for basting. It requires extra work to put a quilt in a frame, but it ensures that the quilt is held evenly while I baste. My frame is made from two-by-fours left over from building our house in Mendocino. It is very sturdy, so I can stand it up to reach the center areas. This is the only reason I can baste on it alone. Otherwise, I would have to roll the quilt, which takes two people. Basting is tedious and a good thing to do with friends. Throw a basting party and give your friends lunch in exchange for their help.

Recently, I added a table surface of 11' x 5' to my studio. We grouped a desk and storage cabinet together for one portion and my husband made a frame of two-by-fours and plywood for the rest — making sure it was all of one height. We covered it all with formica taped at the edges with double-sided tape. Now I baste a quilt up to 11' x 5' on my table.

MARKING

There is great concern in the quilting community over the long-term effects of marking methods. No one knows for sure what will happen with some of the marking pens, so I rely on the traditional methods and artist's drafting tape. My favorite tool is a chalk wheel. It draws a sharp chalk line which is temporary. In fact, I draw the line just

PLATE 7-3.
BEACHWALKERS has been basted in a six-inch grid.

before I quilt it. Chalk pencils can also be used, but be sure you have the type without wax. You can use stencils as templates and trace the design with the chalk pencil just before sewing.

Another marking method which should not damage the quilt is artist's drafting tape. This also needs to be used just before quilting. If it is left on for a time, the tape will leave a residue. Recently, I read in a magazine that a quilter had trouble with tape pulling all the fibers off of the top, so it became thin and worn. I think two things may have happened. She may have used house-painter's masking tape instead of artist's drafting tape. It is much stickier. I suggest going to an art or drafting supply store and buying artist's drafting tape. She may also have used very wide tape. Quilt shops usually have ¼" drafting tape, which would be the best size to use.

When machine quilting with tape as a marking tool, I have found it necessary to put the tape ¼" away from where I want to sew. Then the presser foot follows the edge of the tape. Sewing on top of the tape does not allow the quilt to feed in properly.

Another marking method for machine quilting is to draw the quilting design on paper. Then place the paper on the area to be quilted and quilt through it. This is used for complex designs. There are also products available at quilting stores similar to interfacing that can be removed with water, heat, or pulled off. Some, like the paper, require tedious picking with tweezers to remove all the pieces. I use these only when nothing else will work.

Some pencils can be used if you need to make more permanent markings. The National Quilting Association has reported that regular pencils sometimes have an oil base and are lead rather than graphite, which does not wash out well. Test your pencil before you use it. I have not found it necessary to use pencils for marking. I try to use the elements of the quilt to guide my stitching. If you want to do a design such as a flower on solid fabric, you may need a pencil line.

With all marking methods that require removal, the rule of thumb is to pretest. Use the same fabric used in the quilt and wash it with the same products you will use to wash the finished quilt.

THREAD FOR QUILTING

For all my quilting, I use the best quality thread I can buy. A variety of colors can be used to draw on the quilt. This adds to the color of the quilt and can accent an area which otherwise might be too light or soft. Wrapped core thread frays when used for machine quilting, so use the best quality polyester or cotton thread you can buy.

Some machine quilters like to use nylon thread. I do not like the way it feels. I worry that it will melt if the quilt is washed and put in a dryer. And, I have an aversion to it, after seeing so many photos of seals and other animals injured by nylon fishing line. Since the colored thread adds an exciting dimension to my quilts, the invisible nylon thread is not interesting to me as an artistic element.

MACHINE SETUP

The sewing machine needs to be set up at a comfortable height for working. Put something under the legs of your table if it is too low. You do not want to hunch over the machine for long hours or your back and shoulders will protest. Your chair height should be correct in relation to the table. It may need adjusting also or instead. Your shoulders should not raise uncomfortably while you work.

There needs to be a table at the side and back of the machine to hold the weight of the quilt. Have your threads and scissors handy. If you know you are using one color for a large amount of work, wind several extra bobbins. That way you will not have to stop and do it while you are quilting.

In the photo you can see my setup. The table is ten feet long and three and one-half feet wide. It is white so the table surface does not affect how I see colors. An extra-deep drawer to my right holds all my threads. I pull out the one to my left when working on large quilts to help support the quilt. At eye level I put a board at an angle with the shelf brackets used for magazine racks. On this I keep information for working, inspirational things, or notes on what needs to be done. At one end of the table is a TV so I can work on the machine even when I want to watch. It does not have a remote control, so my husband installed a switch on the audio line so I can block out commercials since they get on my nerves while stitching. If I were having the table made today, I would make two five-foot tables, because they would be easier to move.

Prepare a test quilt using the backing, batting, and top fabric used in your project. Then you can try everything on this sample. Once you have made these preparations, you are ready to begin quilting.

PLATE 7-4. *When I began machine quilting, I had a table built by a cabinetmaker. The machine sits down into the table so there is no drag on the quilt at the needle.*

CHAPTER 8

Machine Quilting

Most of my quilts are quilted by machine because I like the speed of the work and the effect of the stitched line. Machine quilting is usually approached only to imitate traditional quilting. This may be why so many quilters consider it only for speed. Approaching it as another way to enrich the surface of the quilt with thread, color, and line texture opens many new possibilities. There are interesting stitches and methods for varying them that allow you to draw on the quilt with a colored line. (If you already know the basics of machine quilting, you may want to skip forward to the information on line quality.)

I have found even large quilts can be machine quilted. The painted quilt top can be quilted by hand, if you wish, unless the paint was used very thick.

MATERIALS:

SEWING MACHINE

Zigzag capability is necessary for most of the variations. Have the instruction book nearby, as well as attachments and extra needles – everything you need to operate your machine.

THREAD

Select threads the colors of your quilt and medium gray. Wrapped core thread does not work as well as 100% cotton or polyester.

BASIC SEWING SUPPLIES

Scissors, pins, thimble, etc.

BACKING AND BATTING FOR YOUR PROJECT

Allowing extra for a test quilt. See Chapter 7 for a discussion of batting. My current preference is cotton batting.

PLATE 8-1.
HARBOUR SEALS AT MACKERRICKER BEACH, detail, 62" x 66", Vicki L. Johnson. Mendocino, California, © 1981. The quilting lines on this quilt were done very freely with bright colors of thread. The loose line draws the shapes of the landscape, but is not realistically precise.

DARNING FOOT

This foot is for machine embroidery or darning and is available for most machines. If you cannot find a darning foot, try to find a spring needle.

OPTIONAL ITEMS YOU MAY WANT:

OPEN-TOE PRESSER FOOT

You will love this foot if you buy one, but it is optional. Some call it an appliqué foot. It is much easier to see where you are quilting with this foot.

TOP-STITCHING NEEDLE

If you're sewing with metallic thread.

STRAIGHT-STITCH THROAT PLATE

Also for metallic thread.

TRACING PAPER, PENCIL, RULER

For drawing quilting designs.

CHALK WHEEL

Or other chalk device for marking.

TAPE

¼" drafting tape for marking.

MACHINE SETTINGS

Making a small test quilt sandwich using the top fabric, batting, and backing used in your quilt is very helpful in adjusting the machine. It will be necessary for practice if you have never machine quilted.

For most quilts, set the stitch length longer than you normally sew. If you use a 2.5 setting for sewing, use a 3 for quilting. If you use a 12 setting for sewing, use a 10 for quilting. Sew a test line on the sample quilt sandwich and study the tension. If it needs loosening, adjust the top tension and test again until it is making a good stitch. Most good quality machines will not need much adjustment.

If you can set the needle to stay down when you stop, it will be helpful. That way the quilt stays in place as you adjust it for the next movement. This is especially helpful when you do free-motion work. Some machines allow you to reduce the pressure of the presser foot. Try this, if you can, and see if the sandwich feeds under the foot better. When doing free-motion quilting, lower your feed dogs. If you cannot, try stitching with them exposed. If their motion disturbs you, set the stitch length to 0. If the motion of the feed dogs is still a problem, cover them with tape.

For quilting, I usually use regular-weight thread. However, with the machine you can use any type you want. Heavier threads will show more and give more impact to the line. I have been trying silk thread where I want more sheen. Experimenting with threads, just as embroiderers do, will add richness to your work. For further discussion on thread selection, see Chapter 7.

Some machines will not sew properly unless the top and bobbin threads are the same type. Unless you have a machine with this restriction, another interesting effect is to use different threads for top and bobbin. Little dots of bobbin thread appear on the surface. Their color or weight will add a subtle difference to the stitched line.

APPROACH

Just as with hand quilting, it is important to work from the center of the quilt to the edges. If you are doing heavy quilting in the center, this becomes even more important. Thicker batts allow the top to creep. Working from the center eases this creep toward the edge so no puckers form on the front or back of the quilt. You can work from top to bottom, or across the quilt; just do not jump around from space to space. Once a space is firmly held in place by some quilting, you can do some jumping around to add finishing touches.

Continuous designs are easiest to machine quilt. Many starts and stops where you must reposition the quilt are tedious. With small quilts this is not as much of a challenge as with larger ones. For my quilts, I use the design of the top to guide the quilting lines.

Quilting around shapes makes them puff out in relief from the surface. Heavy quilting pushes the area into the background. For the underwater quilts, I stitch around the kelp, seals, and fish so they puff and stand out. They have a rounder contour which

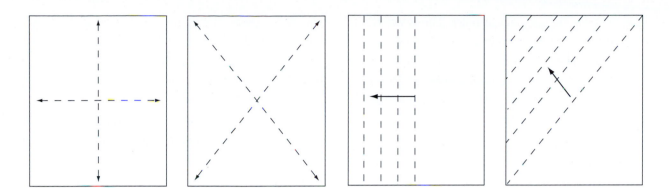

FIGURE 8-1A. *Quilting lines – basic idea.*
For most quilts proceeding out from the center in a manner as shown works best.

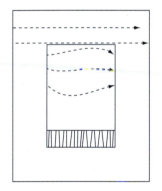

FIGURE 8-1B.
Quilting lines – sample quilt.
STEP 1. *Quilt the painted area first. Start near the center; the tree line is a good place. Then go up into the sky. The long horizontal lines in the rows of squares can also be done.*

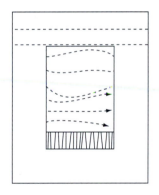

FIGURE 8-1C.
Work down in the painting from your starting place. Not all the details need to be quilted in at this time, just the major areas.

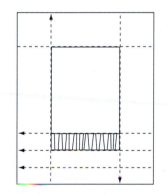

FIGURE 8-1D.
Quilt the long, horizontal line between the painting and the strip. Then work down doing each long horizontal. Next are the long verticals of the painting.

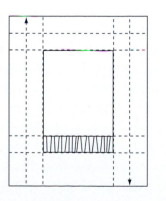

FIGURE 8-1E.
Do the long rows on the side.

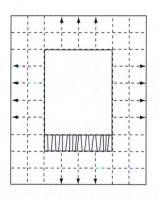

FIGURE 8-1F.
Finish all the short rows. Starting and stopping.

makes it seem like they are in relief. The water has flowing horizontal lines quilted like the motion of water. In the landscape quilts I stitch all around the shapes of the buildings and trees so they stand out. I contour the cliffs by stitching heavily where they recede and less where they stand forward. I quilt the border squares in the ditch.

With the appliqués, you have a choice of stitching over the previously sewn line or around the outside edge. Restitching anchors the fabric again, but going around the outside edge puffs the shape more so it stands out in good relief.

The color of thread you quilt with can make an area stand out or recede. For instance, the tree line against the sky can be softened if quilted with light blue thread to match the sky. It can be emphasized with green thread to match the trees. Another consideration is whether you want a hard edge for an object or a softer one. Thread of the background color will soften the edge. Medium gray thread in a range of tones is useful if you do not have matching thread, or you are unsure what color to choose because of prints, or for areas where you will be moving from one fabric to another. Match the value and tone, (reddish gray or greenish or bluish, etc.)

PLATE 8-2.
Light blue thread that matches the sky, softens this tree line, and makes it recede. The brown tree behind the lighthouse was quilted with a green thread to bring it forward and define the edge.

with value always being the most important when you want to blend into the fabric.

STRAIGHT QUILTING

If you have an open-toe presser foot, use it for the straight quilting. Otherwise, use the foot that allows you to see the needle best. You may be able to use a hacksaw to remove part of the foot in front of the needle to create a foot similar to the open-toe foot.

A very neat beginning or ending is done with three or more very small stitches, (Figure 8-2C) about 14 stitches per inch or a 1 setting on some machines. If you have a computerized machine, sometimes you can program the settings. My machine will remember what was last used when sewing on each number. When the machine is turned off, it returns to its normal settings, so you must do this for each sewing session. On number 1 button, the straight stitch, select the number 3 stitch length and press the number 1 button again. The machine now remembers that stitch length. On number 2 button, the zigzag stitch, select the number 1 stitch length and turn the stitch width to 0. Press the number 2 button again. It now remembers your starting and stopping stitch. All you need do is hop between the two buttons to do the quilting. This saves a lot of time. But remember, you need to reset the buttons if you turn the machine off. When leaving the machine a short time, I just turn off the light. Of course, when leaving a long time, I do turn the whole machine off since reprogramming the buttons is easy. Think about your machine and what would be an easy way to accomplish this so you do not have to reset the stitch length each time.

When ending, cut the top thread first, close to the fabric. Then gently tug on the thread from the back. That buries the short top thread into the batting. You should not pull so hard that you pull out any stitching. Another way to end was shared with me by Nina Miller of Santa Cruz, California. She leaves a longer top thread and pulls it to the back. Then she threads it onto a needle, makes a knot in the thread about one inch from the quilt, and sews into the quilt. Tugging on the thread and easing the knot with your thumbnail buries it in the batting. This is the way some people end hand quilting. This takes longer, but it is a very neat way to end the stitching and can be done without using small ending stitches so they all look the same.

Another way to start the quilting is backstitching three stitches (Figure 8-2B) in an inconspicuous place. The edge of the quilt that will be covered with binding is good. If the straight lines of your design run across the center of the quilt, you can run from edge to edge. Sew the lines crossing the centers first and work up and down from them. See figures 8-1B-F for the pattern used on a quilt similar to the small ones I make.

On patchwork where you want to emphasize the pieced design, quilt in the ditch. Stitch on the single thickness of fabric away from the seams (Figure 8-3). Hold your hands on either side of the needle and keep the quilt taut, but do not stretch it. This is the same position used to sew soft-edge appliqué (Plate 5-8, page 72). Be sure to let the machine feed the quilt under the foot. If you pull the quilt from behind to the front of the foot, the stitching will pucker. Sometimes it is easier to grab the right side of the quilt, or the rolled up part under the machine arm. This is the alternate position used for soft-edge appliqué (Plate 5-9, page 72).

When you cross over an already quilted seam and you can see the fabric of the top is creeping and will form a crease, you can pull both from the front and back to ease the fabric. But this is the only time you should pull like this. If you have basted well, this should seldom be necessary.

If you have never machine quilted, piece a quick sample block and try machine quilting it. This will give you practice with seams before doing your painted quilt or other project. Try to relax while you work. Machine quilting does take practice, especially if you like the slow rhythm of hand quilting. The speed of machine quilting is one of its benefits, but it requires more concentration. Take

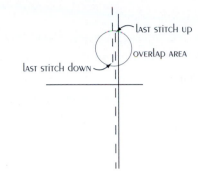

FIGURE 8-2A.
Overlap.

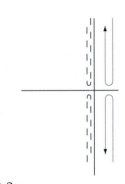

FIGURE 8-2B.
Backstitches.

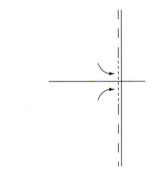

FIGURE 8-2C.
Very small stitches.

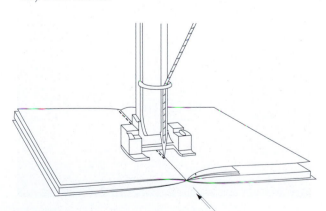

FIGURE 8-3.
Stitching in the ditch.

breaks if you feel yourself tensing. I can only quilt about one and one-half hours at a time, so I like to split up my work sessions. One each in the morning, afternoon, and evening. Four and one-half hours of quilting a day is quite a lot with machine work, but breaking it up allows me to come to it fresh each time.

FREE-MOTION QUILTING

For most of the painted area of a landscape, free-motion quilting works best. Use the darning foot or spring needle for this. If you did the soft-edge appliqué with this foot, the principles are the same. You may want to refer to the free-motion stitching in Chapter 5. If you have a Bernina®, you may want to purchase the open-toe darning foot #24. This foot makes it easier to see your stitching. It also lets you switch feet without cutting the thread, so you can sew a straight line and then change the foot and sew a curvy one.

You will control the stitch length since the darning foot does not feed the fabric. It gives you freedom to move. When the needle is up the foot is up; when the needle is down the foot is down. You can move in any direction, but a good stitch is made.

Some machine instructions say you can stitch without a foot, but it is important to use a foot when quilting. It may be possible to darn with a single layer of fabric, but with all the layers of a quilt it is not. The thickness slows the thread so stitches are skipped. The foot going down presses the layers together, which helps the thread penetrate at a correct speed in relationship to the bobbin hook's movement. This hook must catch the thread to make a stitch.

For free-motion work you can start and stop as for the straight stitching. You can also stitch in place three or four stitches to start or stop. This makes very small stitches locked together knotting the thread. Do not cut off this knot. If you clip the thread that close, you may cut your quilt.

If you have not practiced the free-motion movements before, it is important to do so now. Make a sample quilt sandwich of the same materials used in your quilt and practice on it.

Remember to lower the presser foot even though it will not look lowered. Take a stitch or turn the fly wheel and then pull up the bobbin thread with the top thread. Hold these threads and take three or four starting stitches. Once the thread is locked in the fabric, you can clip these threads. Put your hands to either side of the needle area with the fingers spread forming a hoop. Now you can try moving in any direction. Once you are comfortable with the single stitch, try some of the variations in line quality described in the following section.

When you are quilting over the soft-edge appliqué and you want to follow the same stitching line, the quilting thread sometimes breaks. This happens because the stitching holding the appliqué is so close together. To prevent this, just quilt next to the appliqué stitching line. The effect will be the same. If you do quilt on top of the appliqués, you are reinforcing that stitching by making a second line. I often quilt on top for this reason.

LINE QUALITIES

Before I discovered quiltmaking, one of the things I did was embroidery. With it, you vary the sewn line with the weight and color of thread, and

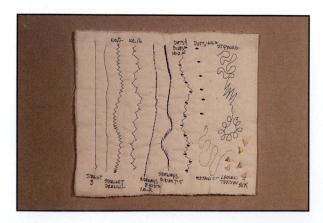

PLATE 8-3.
Various line qualities and stitches.

with the particular stitch you use. I have loved the sewing machine ever since my mother let me make puppets on her brand new machine, so machine embroidery was something I couldn't wait to try once I had my own machine. I learned to vary the machine-sewn line in very much the same way hand stitchers do.

Machine quilting was a natural step for me, but I wanted to vary that sewn line. So I turned to machine embroidery and explored approaching quilting the same way. With embroidery, the stitch was often only decorative and could not actually hold the layers together. Using the approach of embroidery but stitching for quilting, I tried varying the line with different stitch lengths and machine stitches, but kept the tension correct. The results were very exciting. I have just begun to try the different decorative stitches available on the sewing machine – there are many choices.

Moving Sideways

A very thick line of thread can be made by moving sideways while doing the basic satin stitch. Depending on how wide you set the stitch width and how fast you move, more or less thread can be sewn for different thicknesses. If you also move in any direction, but perpendicular to the normal sewing direction, the line will go wider. Once you are sewing in the normal direction, the machine width setting you are using becomes the width of the line. Try this on a sample and move in different directions.

Zigzag Freely

Most machines have a stitch that zigzags at different widths within the same machine setting. This stitch makes an interesting line that loosely follows along in one direction. With free-motion quilting you create the stitch length, so using this stitch you can change from long rambling lines to tight jagged ones, depending on how quickly you move. (See the second row in Plate 8-3.) This varies from quick movements to slower ones and you can see the stitch length change. This stitch is particularly good used in areas such as the cliffs in my Mendocino quilts. The rocky cliffs have jagged edges which are reflected in the line quality of this stitch.

Plate 8-4.
MENDOCINO SPRING, Vicki L. Johnson. Detail of Plate 8-6. The dots on the cliff are done with thread while quilting. If you look closely, you can see I used several different colors of thread which help to enrich the painted color. Areas that recede are quilted more heavily to give dimension to the cliff.

Plate 8-5.
PIGEON PT. BARNS, Vicki L. Johnson. Detail of Plate 1-3, page 11. Different thread colors are used in the cliffs on this quilt. Notice the dots look like bits of rock.

PLATE 8-6. *MENDOCINO SPRING, 42" x 48", Vicki L. Johnson, Soquel, California, © 1992. Photo by George R. Young. When seen in the total quilt, the thread areas become a part of the picture, but without that detail the quilt would not be as interesting.*

DOTS

Dots of thread can be made by using the satin stitch and sewing in place. Secure the thread first by stitching three to four stitches in the same spot. Then change the stitch width and again sew in place. Let the thread build up to the thickness you want, at least four to five widths of thread. Then return to straight stitch width and again secure the stitches by sewing in place three to four times. Used in the cliffs, these dots look like rocks jutting out. (See Plate 8-3, third row.)

You can combine the dots with the jagged line approach. Secure the thread and make a dot, but do not end. Keep the stitch width you selected. Move in any direction letting the needle take one or two stitches. Then stop and make a dot. Now you have dots and lines together. (See Plate 8-3, fourth row.)

STIPPLING

Stippling is very easy and fun to do on the machine. Using the straight stitch first with the free-motion setup, just doodle in a pattern. Try several doodling patterns. It is tempting to do too much sewing, so do not overdo it. When you are trying a sample, a small area is easy to sew heavily. Once you are working on a larger project, all that sewing will take more time. The overall quilting should be done first and then the stippled areas. Heavy stippling draws up the fabric more than usual. Using different colors of thread and stippling offers an opportunity to really affect the color of the quilt with the quilting.

FLOATING SHAPES

Some machines have built-in stitches that can be isolated into shapes (see Plate 8-3, lower right corner). Triangles are floating at different angles. This was done with metallic thread, but could be any color or thread. It would be easy to make rectangles with a zigzag stitch and have them float like these triangles. To do another shape, you will need to play with your machine and its special stitches. Some machines have a built-in button just for

isolating one of these stitches. You will need to read your machine's instruction book to find out how to do it.

METALLIC THREAD

The shimmer of metallic thread adds additional richness to the surface of the quilt. In SUNSET SEA II, (Plate 8-8) I used variegated gold thread to quilt the rays of the setting sun. The thread manufacturer stated that it was for decorative use only, so I did some quilting with regular thread for more strength. With wall quilts, it probably is strong enough by itself.

When I first began to use metallic thread I had difficulty with it breaking or fraying as I stitched, which was very frustrating. Then I learned about top-stitching needles. They have an oval hole that is larger than the standard eye. This makes them easier to use. Other times the thread would break as I went over thick seams. I solved this problem by putting a straight-stitch throat plate on the machine. It keeps the quilt from going down into the hole, so there is no extra tension on the thread and it does not break. This solution only works for straight stitching. You must remember to change throat plates when you use the zigzag stitches or the needle will break.

PLATE 8-7.
SEALS AND GARIBALDIS IN THE THE KELP, Vicki L. Johnson. Detail of Plate 5-18, page 78. I stippled over the whole area of the ocean floor.

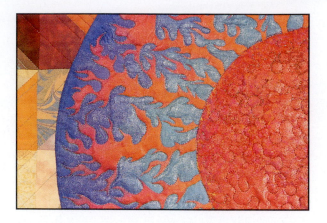

PLATE 8-8.
SUNSET SEA II, Vicki L. Johnson. Detail of Plate 9-2, page 109. Metallic threads add marvelous glitter but are a challenge to use. Both my SUNSET SEA quilts were heavily quilted with it. The suns really sparkle with the red variegated thread.

Use a longer stitch length with the metallic thread so more thread lays on the surface and gives more shine. Test it for tension. You may want to loosen the top tension at least one step. My machine made a good stitch with a regular thread in the bobbin. Again you should test the bobbin thread in your machine as some are fussy. Some stitchers use lingerie thread in the bobbin or very fine polyester thread. Using a bead of Sewer's Aid on the spool of thread also can help if the thread frays. It is a silicon liquid which helps the thread feed through the machine smoothly. It does not leave any mark on the quilt. Check to see if you need a new needle if the thread continues to be a problem.

Experimenting with different colors of bobbin thread along with the metallic top thread gives interesting results. Since I wanted the gold line, I used a gold-colored bobbin thread for SUNSET SEA, (Plate 11-12, page 137). In SUNSET SEA II (Plate 9-2, page 109) I varied the thread colors. Some of the stitching in the sun is with red bobbin and some with blue. That helped contour the sun.

For metallic thread, running the machine too fast causes problems. A steady, rather slow speed works best. Thick areas of paint need careful, slow stitching as it is more difficult for the thread to penetrate.

HINTS FOR USING METALLIC THREAD
- Topstitch needle
- Loosen tension one step, probably two
- Use a longer stitch length
- Try Sewer's Aid
- A steady and rather slow speed
- For straight stitching use a straight-stitch throat plate

QUILTING LANDSCAPES
For the example quilt, BEACHWALKERS, I did not do many stitch variations. Most of the work on the painting was with free-motion quilting. Only in the cliffs did I do variations like the dots. The sky

PLATE 8-9.
Usually I begin quilting a small landscape by first doing the tree line and then working up through the sky.

has free-flowing lines which reflect the motion of the air. The beach is lightly quilted so it puffs up in relief against the other areas. The ocean has lines which are just like wave action. The squares are quilted in the ditch, so they puff up. A more complex quilting in the squares might detract from their repetition of the landscape. One possibility might be to quilt in a continuation of the landscape. Other quilts will need still other approaches to the quilting. Match your quilting to the quilt top's design for the best effect. Check some of the other quilts in this book and in other books for ideas on how other quilt artists have used their quilting to enhance a landscape.

PLATE 8-10.
BEACHWALKERS is now quilted.

CHAPTER 9

BINDING

PLATE 9-1.
Try several fabric strips for the binding. Each binding should make a different area of the quilt stand out. Choose the one that emphasizes the part of the quilt you find most important.

The binding is the final touch to the wall quilt and is very important. Take your time in the selection of the fabric because this can be the part that makes the quilt. Hang your quilt on the wall again. Cut strips of the fabrics you think will be good as bindings. Pin them in place and step back to look. The best choice will suddenly bring out everything you want in the quilt; it will be rather like putting on a dress with just the right colors for you.

MATERIALS:

FABRIC

Read directions to determine yardage

ROTARY CUTTER, RULER, AND MAT.

SELECTION

I find it helps to have another person change the fabric choices while the artist watches. The artist can see immediately which is the best.

It's fun to vary the colors within the binding strips or to use another tuck at the binding. See my quilts SUNSET SEA (Plate 11-12, page 137), SUNSET SEA II (Plate 9-2), and SEA AND SKY TRIAD (Plate 11-8, page 133), as examples of this. In SUNSET SEA II, I used three different colorways of the same print. That enhanced the value change in the water. With SEA AND SKY TRIAD, I put a tucked

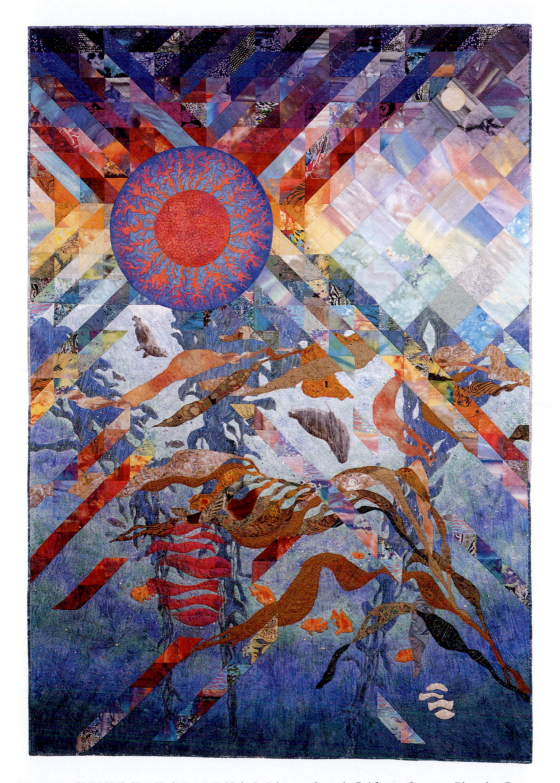

PLATE 9-2. *SUNSET SEA II, 60" x 84", Vicki L. Johnson, Soquel, California, © 1994. Photo by George R. Young. Where the design of the quilt suggested the border change color, I used a different colorway of the same print. I used a forty-five degree diagonal to sew the binding strips together so the line on the binding would not be different from the lines on the quilt. The colors change from light to dark in this quilt, so one fabric for the binding did not work. I used three colorways of the same print. At the top is the lighter one, with the darkest on the bottom. At the points where the color values changed, I joined the two at an angle.*

FIGURE 9-1.
Double fabric binding. Cut a strip 2½" wide for a ½" finished binding. Press in half, wrong sides together.

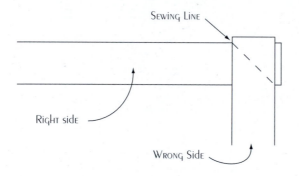

FIGURE 9-2.
Joining two strips. Place right sides together and perpendicular to each other. Sew across the corner at a forty-five degree angle.

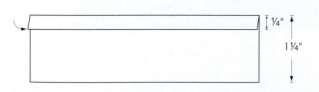

FIGURE 9-3.
Single fabric binding. Cut a strip 1½" wide for a ½" finished binding.

edge at the binding. When I tried the different fabrics for the binding, I could not decide between two, so I used both.

In my experience, bias binding is not necessary. Using the straight grain helps to keep the edges flat. It is important to use bias binding if you have curved edges. It is the only type that will lie flat.

For my quilts, I use two different binding methods. Some quilts need a very firm binding; for those I do a doubled fabric binding. This is the one I see most quilters using. On smaller quilts, or when I am short on fabric, I use a single layer of binding fabric. This is not as firm and should only be used when the quilt is very flat and square. Because it gives a stronger edge, a doubled binding can help square up the quilt.

DOUBLE FABRIC BINDING

To do the doubled fabric binding, decide how wide you want the bound edge to be when finished. Double this figure and add a seam allowance of ¼". Then double that measurement. For most of mine I want ½" showing so the formula is: ½"+ ½"+ ¼" = 1¼". Then I double that figure to have a total of 2½". This is the measurement I use to cut strips for binding fabric (see Figure 9-1). A narrower edge is nice on small quilts and can be achieved by using a total of 1¾" or 2" to make a binding a bit more than ¼".

Using the rotary cutter, cut enough strips to go all the way around the quilt. On small quilts I do not join the strips together, but use one full length on each side. This does waste some fabric, but I use the fabric later in strip piecing.

JOINING STRIPS

For larger quilts, I piece the strips together on the diagonal. Lay two strips, right sides together, perpendicular to each other. Sew across the diagonal of the intersection of the two (see Figure 9-2). Trim the seam to a bit less than ¼" and iron it open. You can make a continuous strip of fabric as long as the circumference of your quilt, plus a little extra for the corners. Iron this strip in half with the right sides of the fabric out for doubled fabric binding. Use the same method to join strips for single-fabric binding.

I do not miter corners. Amish quilters, who are considered excellent craftswomen, do not miter so I have decided that if they do not, I do not have to either.

SINGLE FABRIC BINDING

For a single-layer binding, the cutting formula is: the width of the finished binding edge + seam allowance x 2. For my small quilts I usually use: ½" + ¼" x 2 = 1½" . This is the width of the strip I would cut. Again, on a small quilt I do not piece the binding.

For this binding, I press a ¼" folded edge along the whole length of the strip (see Figure 9-3). This forms a finished edge to hand sew on the back of the quilt. The sewing procedure is the same for both of these bindings.

SEWING

If you stitched along the quilt's edge while basting, you are ready to apply the binding. Make sure the top has not pushed beyond the basted edge so you have a bulge. If so, remove the edge basting and resew it. If you did not baste the edge originally, it will help to do so now. You can machine baste with less than a ¼" seam.

Use the edge of the quilt as a guide to sew on the binding. Match the cut, unfolded edge of the binding strip to the quilt top edge. Measure opposite sides of the quilt and decide what length the quilt will be, if the measurements are not the same. Usually, the measurement closest to the planned size is best. With a pin, mark this measurement on the binding strip. Do not cut the fabric to length before it is sewn. Pin the binding in place, stretching or easing it if necessary to make the binding fit. Sew the binding to the quilt, right sides together, using the quilt top edge as a guide. You may have to ease the binding a bit so no folds form. With the

PLATE 9-3.
Sew the binding onto the sides of the quilt with a ¼" seam.

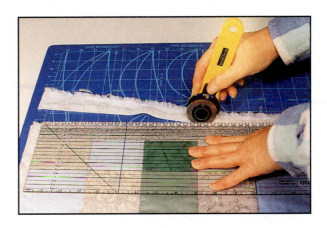

PLATE 9-4.
Remove the excess batting by trimming with a rotary cutter.

PLATE 9-5.
The Amish quilters finish corners with this method.

double binding this is especially important because there are so many layers of fabric. Sew through both cut edges of the doubled binding.

Sew the vertical sides first and then the horizontal. The top and bottom edges then contain the side edges of the quilt, keeping it from visually flowing up or down into space.

After the two vertical sides are sewn, trim away excess backing and batting, keeping ½" (or your binding width) as filler in the edge. An easy way to trim the excess is with your rotary cutter, ruler, and mat. Lay the quilt with the excess to your right (if you are right handed), place the ruler with ¼" (if you want a different width binding, adjust for your size) measured beyond the cut edge of the binding and trim with the rotary cutter (see Plate 9-4).

Remove the basting stitches sewn along the vertical edges. Turn the quilt over and pin the folded edge of the binding just over the machine stitching line. Hand sew the folded edge down with an appliqué stitch.

Repeat for the top and bottom, but leave a ¼" piece at each end. Fold in this extra piece while pinning to finish the corner. Close the end with a slip stitch.

THOUGHTS ON PHOTOGRAPHY

Although the quilt is finished, I do not consider it complete until it is ready to hang. In the next chapter I will discuss hanging methods. I like to keep a photographic record of all my quilts, so I do not consider them finished until they have been photographed. Even if you do not want to share the photos with anyone, photographs give you a chance to see how your work has progressed. This is important in your development as an artist. By reviewing the work you have done, you may understand yourself better. This will help you know what you do best, so you can develop it further. It takes time to develop your own visual language. Studying your own work can help you.

PLATE 9-6.
*BEACHWALKERS, 24" x 30", Vicki L. Johnson, Soquel, California © 1994.
The completed quilt now needs only a hanging device and storage bag.*

Chapter 10

Hanging, Care, Storage, and Shipping

A wall quilt's construction does not end with the binding. It still needs to be prepared for hanging. In this chapter I will tell you how I hang my quilts and give you some information about care, storage, and shipping.

HANGING

Once a wall quilt is finished, hanging it is quite simple. What is referred to as a sleeve is sewn onto the back near the top. It is a nice touch to use the same fabric as the backing for the sleeve. Some

artists even go to creative lengths to make the sleeve a part of the back art if they have done some. Then a wooden strip is slipped into the sleeve. To weight the quilt on the bottom to help it hang flat, a sleeve and stick can also be sewn near the bottom in the same manner. Only for large quilts do I find this necessary; small ones do not need it.

For quilt shows, a four-inch sleeve is often required to meet hanging requirements. A sleeve this wide is necessary only if the quilt is going to be exhibited. Sometimes I attach a four-inch muslin sleeve over my permanent one for those quilts I expect to exhibit. Then when the quilt is retired from showing, the muslin sleeve can be removed.

When hung permanently, placement of the quilt is very important. Too much light can damage textiles in a very short time. Walls that the sun hits at any time of day are not suitable. A wall without direct light is best. Even artificial lightning can damage textiles over time. Try not to aim a light directly at the quilt or so close that its heat gets to the quilt. Fluorescent lights are also damaging. In all types of lighting, it is the ultraviolet light which damages fiber. Sometimes filters can be obtained to keep out the UV light.

Textile conservationists recommend rotating your quilt collection so each quilt hangs for only

PLATE 10-1.
The stick needs a little extra space in the sleeve so the quilt does not pucker where the sleeve is attached.

PLATE 10-2. *PIGEON PT. AND SANDPIPERS, 4' x 6', Vicki L. Johnson, Soquel, California, © 1994. Photo: Charley Lynch. Quilts are flexible and work in situations where paintings do not. It would be fun to have this quilt of a lighthouse hanging on a round wall. A curved piece of aluminum could be used in place of a wooden stick for hanging.*

six months at a time. This allows the fibers to rest and regain their shape. This is particularly important for the more fragile older quilt. My quilts at home have been hanging for several years and I have not had any problems. I do not know what more time will do to them. You have to judge for yourself how much risk you wish to take in order to enjoy your quilts. Putting them away in a drawer for someone else to enjoy years later may not make sense unless they are meant to be an inheritance.

Round poles make the quilt bulge at the top. This is disturbing to me, so I use flat wood strips. That way the quilt hangs flat against the wall with no hanging device showing. If the device shows, you must consider it part of the piece when planning the total effect. Poorly made hanging devices drastically detract from the quilt.

SLEEVE CONSTRUCTION

Before making a permanent sleeve, acquire a wooden strip. Measure the top of the finished quilt, including binding, and have the wood strip cut ½" shorter. Do not think that you used 24" as the measurement while working and added a ½" binding, so you need 24½". This will be too wide since the quilting has taken up some of the width. It will probably now be more like 23½" wide. Take this

measurement to the lumber store and they will cut the strip to size for you.

Today, most lumber stores are self-serve. Go to the molding area and pick your own. If this is totally foreign to you, ask for help. Just think how a man might feel the first time in a quilt shop finding fabric. I have found most lumber store employees to be quite helpful. For small quilts I use a pine lath which measures 1⅜" wide and ¼" thick. For quilts wider than 36", I use a lath 1¾" wide. The additional width keeps it from bowing from the weight of the quilt. These measurements are actual and not the "before finishing" sizes the lumber store will be using, so take a small ruler to measure the finished width of the lath.

Have the lath cut to your specified length and you will only pay for what you need. They do have the same type of minimums quilt stores have. Usually, you pay in foot increments and they will not let you leave a piece measuring less than four feet. If you are handy around wood, you can buy extra lath and cut it at home as you need it. I use a framer's miter box to cut the lath. After cutting, drill a small hole, about ⅛" diameter, in each end, close to the edge. If you have no drill available, very small screw eyes can be used. Screw them into the top edge at the ends. They must be small or they will split the wood.

Once you have the lath home, sand both ends smooth. Then sand all sides a bit to remove any dirt. Put the sandpaper in your hand and wrap it around the stick. Run the strip through your hand a few times. This will remove the sharp edges and hopefully any potential edge splinters. Use a damp paper towel or rag to clean off all the sanding dust.

You can use the strip this way and no further work is required. As long as you use a wood such as pine or fir, you can get away with not sealing the lath, but it is much better to seal the wood. If for some reason you want to stain the wood, (not necessary or desirable if it does not show) then you must seal it. It would be best to cover all your lath with a urethane plastic varnish. This is very impor-

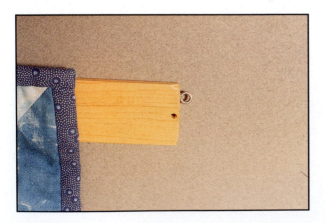

PLATE 10-3.
Screws must be small and screwed into the end of the stick as the wood splits easily.

tant for older quilts. Contact with the wood is harmful to the fabric over time.

Once you have the lath, you can make the sleeve. Measure the width and thickness of the lath. Use the following formula: width + thickness of the lath x 2 + ¾" = width of strip of fabric to cut. This has ¼" added for ease around the stick. Cut a strip of fabric this wide and as long as your quilt is wide plus an inch. Fold one short edge over ¼" and sew. To find the exact length, place the strip onto the back at the top of your quilt. Position it with the sewn edge ½" in from the quilt edge. Fold over the unsewn short end at the point which is ½" from the other side of the quilt. Finger press and sew; then trim the excess (see Plate 10-4).

Fold the sleeve lengthwise, wrong sides together, bringing one long side to within ¼" of the other long side (see Plate 10-5). Press. This fold is well creased. Now position the raw edges exactly together and using the machine, sew them with a ¼" seam. Place the raw edges of the sleeve at the top of the quilt, aligning the seamline just below the binding. The cut edges face the bottom of the quilt – the folded edge will extend above the quilt. The short creased side should be up. By hand, with a running stitch, sew the sleeve to the quilt just below the binding. If you are hanging a fragile older quilt, use small stitches and go through all layers, just catching the front layer. A new quilt can be done this way, or sewn just at the edge of the binding, catching the back and a bit of batt.

Fold the sleeve down onto the quilt and smooth. At the pressed crease smooth the fabric so the short side fits to the back to make the next sewing line. This leaves some room for the thickness of the lath. Then whipstitch the bottom edge of the sleeve at the crease. While doing this, also sew the ends nearest the quilt to the backing. That way the lath won't be accidently slipped between the sleeve and the quilt.

Now you should have a sleeve that fits your lath. Slide the wood strip in and hang your quilt. Small nails through the holes in the lathe or the

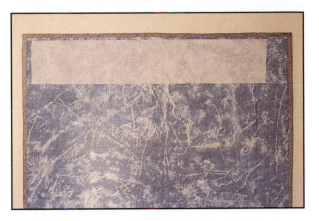

PLATE 10-4.
The length of the sleeve can be measured by placing the fabric, with one end finished, onto the quilt at the top. Fold over the unfinished end and finger press. Then sew this edge to finish and trim the excess length.

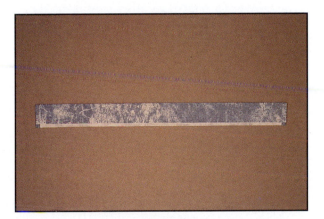

PLATE 10-5.
To make an ease allowance in the sleeve, fold the fabric lengthwise to within ¼" of the other side. Then iron to form a crease to guide you later in sewing.

PLATE 10-6.
Match the unfinished edges and sew with a ¼" seam allowance.

screw eyes should be all that is necessary to hang the quilt. Be sure the wall you choose is not in direct sun. Textiles are like watercolors, they cannot take direct sun or they fade. A very bright sunny room is not the best choice for hanging a quilt or any other textile.

HOOK TAPE AND FRAME

For a permanent installation, an alternate hanging method can be used that supports all edges of the quilt. This is especially good for fragile fibers. Hook tape (for example: VELCRO®) is attached to the quilt on a cotton twill tape backing. It is important to use a backing tape for the hook tape as some quilters have reported that fabric has disintegrated under the hook tape. The other side of the hook

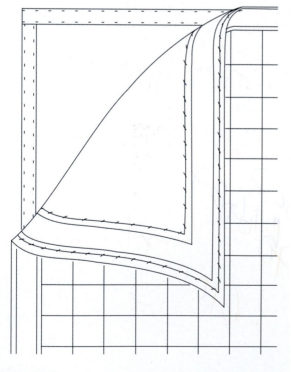

FIGURE 10-1.

Hanging with hook tape. Back of tape stapled to wall or frame. Other side of hook tape sewn to cotton twill tape, which is sewn to the quilt.

tape is stapled to a wooden frame made just the size of the quilt or directly to the wall. Then the quilt can be pressed onto the frame.

IRREGULAR SHAPES

Quilts with irregular-shaped tops can be hung with still another method. Plywood or foam-core board can be slipped into a pocket, which is sewn to the back of the quilt. The pocket needs to follow the irregular shape of the top of the quilt. Lay the top portion of the quilt onto a large piece of paper. Draw its shape onto the paper to make a pattern. After you have drawn the top shape connect the two edges with a straight line which will be the bottom edge of the pocket. You may need to extend the vertical sides a bit if the shaping is only along the top (thinking in terms of an upside-down pocket may help). Add a seam allowance. Using the pattern as a guide, cut two layers of fabric with right sides together. Finish off the straight edges of the fabric by folding the seam allowance up and stitching. Put the right sides together again and sew the irregular edges and vertical sides together. Turn and iron. You should have a pocket. Now sew the irregular edge to the quilt back with a whipstitch. It can be stitched just below or on the backside of the binding. Also sew the straight edge down that is closest to the quilt so no one can accidentally put the hanger next to the quilt.

Cut a piece of foam-core board or plywood to the same shape as your paper pattern minus seam allowance. This will be your hanger. In the center of the hanger, about six inches down from the top, make two holes all the way through the stiff piece so you can slip a heavy thread through. With the hanger in the pocket, sew a heavy thread through the pocket fabric and the hanger's holes. If the quilt is heavy you may want to go through twice for added strength. Tie the ends to make a loop. This will be for hanging onto a nail. If you use foam-core board you should be aware that archival quality board is available. It is unknown how the foam-core board and the quilt will react in time, but archival quality would be safest. For a long-term solution a piece of urethane coverd wood would be better.

CLEANING

Most wall quilts will not need much cleaning. Every few months I vacuum the top edge where some dust accumulates. About once a year I shake my quilts. You can place them in a cool dryer for a few minutes to remove dust if your quilt is really dusty. I live in the country with two big dogs and have my windows open every moment possible, so not many houses could be dustier than mine. Over several years, I have not found that anything more than light vacuuming has been necessary for my wall quilts.

Since all my fabrics are prewashed and the painted pieces have been washed, all my quilts are washable. To me this is very important. Many quilt artists seem to take the view that the quilts will never be washed. That may be quite true, but I believe they should be washable. I never know

PLATE 10-7. *BRIGHT WINTER DAY IN MENDOCINO, 65" x 82", Vicki L. Johnson, Mendocino, California, © 1985. Photo by George R. Young. This quilt has been washed twice. None of the small appliqué pieces are even loose. New quilts survive washing better than older ones, but wallhangings should only be washed when absolutely necessary.*

what someone who owns one of my pieces will decide to do, even with directions attached on the back. Much of my time and effort has been put into making these pieces, so I feel spending a little extra time to help them last is worth the trouble.

The method textile conservationists recommend for washing quilts is very laborious. In the appendix there is a textile conservation pamphlet listed from the American Quilt Study Group in San Francisco. Send for this pamphlet if you would like directions for washing a fragile older quilt.

Never dry clean a quilt or other fragile textile. The dry-cleaning process subjects the textile to very high heat in order to remove the dry-cleaning chemicals, so it is very hard on the fibers. Some larger cities may have cleaners who specialize in handling precious textiles.

When I do wash one of my quilts, I use the washing machine. Because they are new, and I seldom wash them, this so far has not seemed to be harmful. Using Orvus® soap and a very light agitation, machine washing has not harmed A BRIGHT WINTER DAY IN MENDOCINO (Plate 10-7). Because it is light-colored and has been exhibited frequently, I have needed to wash it twice.

Orvus® is available at feed stores in large quantities. Sixteen-ounce containers are available and

easier to handle, but per ounce are expensive. I bought one small and one large. When the little container is empty, I just refill it from the big one. For one quilt, five tablespoons was suggested in an article about washing quilts, but seems excessive in my experience. For smaller loads, such as the fabrics, I have been using one tablespoon.

A friend of mine was making a quilt that was basted heavily, but had gotten dirty from cats sleeping on it. We discussed whether she could safely wash it by machine. I recommended she skip the agitation steps and use a new plumber's friend (the tool you plunge a toilet with) to force the water through the quilt, then let the machine drain and spin the water out. It worked beautifully. This is now the method I will use to wash my quilts.

ROLLING THE QUILT

Have you ever seen a lovely quilt with a permanent crease down the center? This can be avoided by rolling the quilt for storage. Most textiles can be rolled onto tubes and placed on a shelf or top of a cabinet. All of my quilts, even one 82" wide, are stored this way. If you cannot find enough space to place the quilt rolled full width, fold it in thirds or half and then roll it. When folding, acid-free paper or other padding should be placed along the fold to keep it from creasing (see Plate 10-8).

In times past, all quilts not in use were stacked onto the spare bed for flat storage. Most of us do not have an extra bed to do this, so some smaller area is necessary. I find rolling them to be the best solution.

It is very, very important to roll quilts with the face out so the quilted areas do not become squished and wrinkled. Quilters seem not to have learned this basic textile storage concept. When I ship a quilt to a quilt show, it usually returns with the face rolled in, even when I send directions clearly requesting it be rolled with the face out. At shows where weavers or artists are in charge, my quilts return rolled correctly. It is necessary for the preservation of our work that quilters become

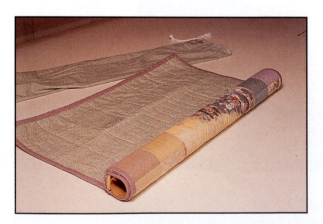

PLATE 10-8.
If quilts are not stored flat, they should be rolled with the top facing out, then placed in a bag or wrapped with fabric.

aware of the proper care of textiles.

If your quilt is rolled wrong side out, and it becomes wrinkled on the face, the wrinkles can be removed by blocking. Sometimes all you have to do is lay the quilt on a bed for a few days and the wrinkles will disappear. Other times, hanging it will do the same thing. In worst cases actually blocking the quilt will be necessary. I stretch the quilt on my pinup wall with pins every three inches around the quilt. Be sure to have it squared or you will block it out of shape. Next, spray it with water until the whole quilt is evenly wet. Then wait until the quilt is totally dry, usually overnight, to remove the pins. This should take out the wrinkles. This method can also be used to straighten a quilt distorted in quilting.

PREPARATION FOR STORAGE OR SHIPPING

After a quilt is ready for hanging, I prepare it for storage or shipping. I find a cardboard tube slightly longer than the full width of the quilt. It is best to have acid-free tubes. If the quilt is to be stored longer than the time to ship to a show, covering the tube with muslin or acid-free paper is important. The quilt, rolled face out on the tube, is then slipped into a fabric bag to keep the quilt clean.

Never store a quilt in a plastic bag. I have heard too many horror stories about quilts going to the garbage dump because they were in plastic bags. It is also not a good practice because plastic holds in moisture and the quilt cannot breathe. Mildew can grow on it under these conditions. The rolled quilt should be kept at the same temperature you like to live in, not in the basement or attic. It should be away from extremes of temperature and humidity.

BAG CONSTRUCTION

A simple bag made from the fabric used on the backing or one that co-ordinates with the quilt can be constructed for storage. The matching is not necessary, but helps to find a quilt when there are several. It is also part of the finishing touch that craftspeople add to their work.

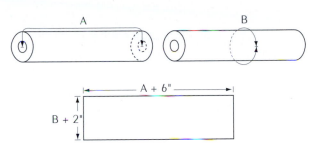

FIGURE 10-2A.
Storage bag construction steps. All measurements are done with quilt rolled around tube. From center of tube over quilt to other center and around quilt. Fabric – Cut to: A+6" x B+2".

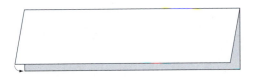

FIGURE 10-2B.
Fold right sides together.

FIGURE 10-2C.
Sew across end and up side with ¼" seam. stop 6" from other end.

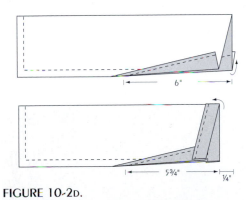

FIGURE 10-2D.
Fold each edge over ¼" and sew to finish.

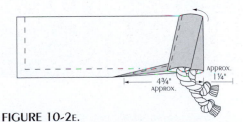
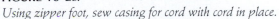

FIGURE 10-2E.
Using zipper foot, sew casing for cord with cord in place.

The bag is made from a rectangle six inches longer than the width of the rolled quilt (measuring from the center of the tube down the length of the tube to the center of the tube at the other end) (see Figure 10-2A) and two inches wider than the circumference of the rolled quilt. Fold the fabric in half lengthwise, right sides together. Sew along the bottom and up to within 6" of the top using a ¼" seam allowance. Then fold over ¼" on the remaining seam allowance to finish each edge up to the top. Fold over a ¼" edge finish at the top and sew, or plan your initial cutting to have the selvage at the top. Lay a cord on the top and fold over the edge until you have a casing for the cord. With your zipper foot, sew this casing along the edge previously sewn. This will make a simple bag to store the rolled quilt.

SHIPPING

When shipping any quilt, prepare it as for storage. Then purchase a box as long as the rolled quilt and square enough to comfortably fit the circumference. For instance, I make many quilts 24" x 30". These take a box 24" x 8" x 8". Most shops that do shipping can sell you a box of this dimension or up to 48" long. When I need one longer, I sandwich two together or cut down a found box. Sometimes you can find great boxes for longer quilts discarded at sport shops or drapery stores. They are used to ship skis and blinds.

Place the rolled quilt in a plastic bag for shipping. This is the only time a quilt should be put into plastic. My son has worked for a shipping service and told me how dirty a sorting room can be. Dust can work into your box, so your quilt should be protected. The plastic bag will also keep any moisture away if the box is exposed to rain or snow.

When I ship a quilt I never mark quilt on the box. People are becoming aware of the value of quilts, so we must become aware of protection methods. I insure my quilts and I use a service that requires a signature upon receipt. This makes a person responsbile for accepting delivery. To insure your quilt you will be asked to prove the value you claim. An appraiser can do this for you. A list of certified appraisers can be obtained from the American Quilter's Society. With an appraisal, you can also add the quilt on a rider to your house insurance. This is a good idea if you intend to exhibit it.

More of us need to become aware of the importance of rolling our quilts face out for storing and shipping. It would delight me if quilt show organizers and their staffs would become aware of this method for packing. It would save trying to steam out wrinkles on the face of the quilt when it returns. Try rolling a small piece face in and you will see exactly what I mean.

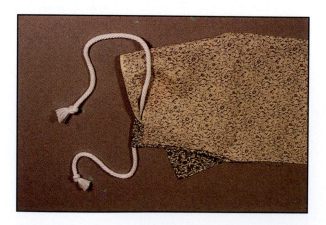

PLATES 10-9.
Here you can see the cording at the end of the bag as it is being sewn.

SECTION III

DESIGNING
YOUR OWN QUILTS

Chapter 11

Expansion into Larger Quilts

Many people who have never painted before, but who have an adventuresome spirit, have been in my classes. This is the same spirit with which to approach a larger project.

The challenge with the painted fabric is in combining it with other more traditional methods of quilting. The excitement for the artist is in this challenge and in the results. The juxtaposition of the painted fabric with commercially printed fabric makes a much richer surface.

THINKING BIGGER

In this book, I presented you with the idea of doing a small landscape wall quilt as the learning project. Just capturing a loved landscape can be a challenging and satisfying project. This may be all you want to do, as it is for many artists, but there are more possibilities beyond the realistic painting.

With a larger work, the same overall concept can be used. A realistic landscape works in the smaller size or somewhat larger, but it is difficult to do more elaborate ideas in a small space. However, large quilts can also be made from simple ideas. The rich surface is very exciting and makes a simple concept exciting in a larger quilt. In fact, a simple concept can work best. For BEACHWALK (Plate 4-3, page 56), I wanted to show the open airy feeling of being on a beach in Mendocino. I put triangles in the sky to represent birds to help with this concept. The whole quilt was created to reflect that vision.

A more elaborate idea is done in my quilt THE NEXT FRONTIERS II (Plate 11-1). At this time, exploration of both space and sea is taking place. Using sea and space together on a quilt seemed an intriguing concept. I also hoped it would be a metaphor for the exploring that individuals are doing. It is not necessary that each viewer understand my second layer of meaning. Some on reflection will understand it and may find something more in the successful work. Many times after I have finished a piece, I learn from the work more of what I was saying. Even years later I can have an insight about an earlier quilt. Sometimes I learn from the viewers' reactions.

While showing slides of my work to people in Mendocino, I said the logs on the beaches were really taking over, but I did not know what they might symbolize. One of the viewers spoke up and said they were just like the people here, washed up on the beaches with no farther to go. It seemed right to me, but it was her interpretation. Viewers bring their own experiences to the work and help complete it.

One thing which helped me in designing was

PLATE 11-1. *THE NEXT FRONTIERS II, 42" x 48", Vicki L. Johnson, Mendocino, California, © 1989. Photo by George R. Young. The combination of painting and piecing helps this quilt with its message. The sky, or space, was pieced with the painted planets appliquéd on top. Austrian crystal beads form the constellations of the winter sky. The sea is painted with soft-edge appliqué kelp.*

PLATE 11-2 (TOP LEFT). *MENDOCINO FOGBANK,*
80" x 60", Vicki L. Johnson, Mendocino, California,
© 1985. Photo by George R. Young. For this scene of
Mendocino, I wanted the fog to flow across the town, just
as the creative spirit flows through the community of artists.
The panels on the side repeat the foggy and sunny colors.

PLATE 11-3 (BOTTOM LEFT). *BARN AT SUNSET,*
37" x 37", Vicki L. Johnson, Soquel, California, © 1993.
Private collection. Photo by George R. Young. When I started
this barn painting, I intended to use squares worked into the
painted areas as I had on the HAUN BARN (Plate 1-10,
page 23). However, the painting turned out so well, I did
not want to break into it too much. Then I thought of a
handkerchief I inherited from my mother with ¼" squares
appliquéd as a border. Perhaps squares could be used in
the same manner on my barn. It worked beautifully.

PLATE 11-4. *THE HAUN BARN REMEMBERED, 6' x 4', Vicki L. Johnson, Soquel,*
California, © 1991. Collection of the Valley Oak Dental Group, Manteca, California.
Photo by George R. Young. This is the same barn used in several other barn quilts, but
on a sunny day. Barn swallows are flying in the sky (the gray triangles), and one flies
over the meadow, which I painted. The sky was created using the same approach as in
A BRIGHT WINTER DAY IN MENDOCINO (Plate 10-7, page 119). Again, I
used squares within the meadow area to blend the painting and piecing.

becoming more aware of the meaning of symbols. The book *Man and His Symbols* by Carl Jung opened a new understanding of the response everyone has to certain forms as symbols. A painting of a fish can be just that, but it is also a symbol in many cultures with different meanings. Combined with other elements, more layers of meaning can be suggested.

Creative thinking is often just combining two different things the artist has never before seen together. This can be anything – ideas or designs or both. The small squares floating inside the edge of the painting, but creating a frame on my BARN AT SUNSET (Plate 11-3) and PIGEON PT. AND SANDPIPERS (Plate 10-2, page 115), were inspired by a handkerchief I inherited from my mother. In college I remember reading a definition of creativity as putting two things together that had not been put together before. Looked at that simply, creating is not difficult.

Do not be intimidated by original design. Everyone is creative. Some have been practicing it more, and it does take practice. It is hard work whether you are experienced or not. Once you have worked with your own ideas, you will not want to return to copying others. Your own work is much more satisfying.

BEGINNING TO DESIGN

First, conceptualize your quilt. Try to visualize it in your mind without being concerned about how you will accomplish it. Your mind can redesign a composition instantly which would take you hours to draw. Often, I think about this stage just before or after sleep. The mind is very creative then, because the right brain can take precedence. When you are fully awake your left-side analytical thinking takes over. Find times when you can daydream about your quilt. In school we were often criticized for daydreaming, so we have to practice doing it now. Right-brain thinking is not often encouraged in school.

Once you have the idea firmly in mind, doodle or sketch, rearranging the elements. If graph paper

does not inhibit you, draw on it. Then draw the major elements in scale, if you have not already been working to scale. Decide on a module before you start. I usually use three inches. A module helps you build each element in relationship to the others. Just because you select three inches does not mean everything has to be in multiples of three – 1½", 4½", or any number that divides or multiplys or adds from the original module can be used. Remember you are in control; if you want to vary you can.

Tissue paper is a designer's best friend. You can lay it over a design and make changes on top, using the parts that were successful. If your design has many repeats, draw one repeat and use the copy machine to make more. That way you do not have to draw each one. After several of these thumbnail sketches, you should arrive at the best composition.

My sketches are usually no more than the ones in Figure 11-1. If you like to plan more on paper, go ahead. Once I know the overall elements, I start on the fabric. Sometimes the quilt takes over and tells me it needs to be a different size. Then I change the plan to accommodate what is happening in the quilt. While making BARN AT SUNSET (Plate 11-3), I was planning to put squares into the meadow and sky as I had done with an earlier quilt, THE HAUN BARN (Plate 1-10, page 23) and THE HAUN BARN REMEMBERED (Plate 11-4). However, the painting turned out so well I did not want to cover it with that many squares. It still needed enriching with other fabrics, so I thought of the design on my mother's handkerchief and came up with the floating square border. My usual 3" squares did not work because the proportions were off, so I had to adapt the design and use 2" squares.

COMBINING METHODS

Once you know the basic composition, you can begin to think about techniques. Large open areas such as my seas are good as painted backgrounds. For landscapes, the organic elements are candidates for painting. Buildings or manmade objects stand out and can be appliquéd.

Skies can be painted or combined with piecing. For my larger Mendocino quilts, I painted a sky first. Then I created a pieced sky with a jagged bottom edge and holes in it. I laid this over the painted sky and carefully pinned. The two were then hand appliquéd together. The result looks like I pieced the painted sky into the patchwork sky (Plate 10-7, page 119).

Elements that you want to look more realistic can also be painted. In THE NEXT FRONTIERS II (Plate 11-1, page 125), I wanted the viewer to know which planets they were seeing. The planets could have been made from marbled fabric, but the viewer would have had no more than a sense of "planetness." So I chose to paint the planets.

Large background areas can also be pieced, like the space on THE NEXT FRONTIERS II. For this, I pieced a pinwheel "space" of navy and dark fabrics. Then I hand appliquéd the planets onto the pieced background. Since I knew where I was going to put the planets, underneath the larger ones I only pieced in a muslin backing, but made sure the piecing would extend under the planets. Once the appliqué was complete, I cut away the backing fabrics. Under the smaller planets, the piecing continued and there were bulky seams under them. By planning to cut the underlying fabric away under the larger planets, I eliminated bulky seams and the planets are flat. But too much planning can be inhibiting and difficult to execute. If I had tried to use muslin under all the planets, I would have been committed to place the smaller planets in exact locations. By continuing the piecing, I could rearrange the smaller planets once I had them to play with.

Always give yourself flexibility. The "fudge factor" is very important in making quilts. I do not make myself decide on the size or placement of an element until I can see the total quilt. By leaving extra fabric, or continuing the piecing under the planned appliqué, I can change the composition as I

FIGURE 11-1.
Thumbnails of THE NEXT FRONTIERS II. These are from my sketchbook and are typical of the drawings I do before beginning a quilt.

work. Having a pinup wall, or some means of placing the sections to see them vertically, is essential. All elements need to be created and placed in position before the final sewing. If you sew too soon, you may find a need to rip in order to correct the composition. Living with the work in flux, where you see it during your day, allows you to think about it. Being able to see it from different distances also helps you see problem areas and the solutions.

SERIES QUILTS

Doing more than one quilt from a concept can be interesting. It lets you develop the idea several ways or improve it. Once you have finished a quilt, you usually know how to improve it. Ideas grow from each other. While you are working, keep a record of the thoughts which develop. You can see the progression in my quilts with NIGHT BEACONS (Plate 11-5) and NIGHT BEACONS III

PLATE 11-5. *NIGHT BEACONS, 36" x 52", Vicki L. Johnson, Soquel, California, © 1989. Private collection. The first of my night beacon quilts was inspired by Bobby Dolph, who was making six-inch star blocks in red, white, and blue for a quilt for her bed. They so intrigued me that I wanted to make some, but decided to do them in my usual three-inch module so they could fit into larger navy stars. I used only blues and whites like the night sky. The bottom border was chosen because it reflected the movement of the waves. Later I learned it is called Big Dipper, a most appropriate choice for this star quilt.*

PLATE 11-6. *NIGHT BEACONS III, 48" x 70", Vicki L. Johnson, Soquel, California, © 1992. Collection of the Museum of the American Quilter's Society, Paducah, Kentucky. Photo courtesy of the Museum of the American Quilter's Society. Since the small version was a success, I decided to expand it. This time I used 4½" and 6" star blocks in addition to the 3" ones and added dark purples and teals to my sky colors. In the light of the lighthouse beacon, I fractured the evening star block. This is actually the third version. The second is very similar to this one, but it does not have as much color and the lighthouse does not have lights in the small entry building or the reflection painted on the tower.*

(Plate 11-6). When the first was finished, I knew the concept was worth enlarging, so I did another. NIGHT BEACONS III has larger and more varied stars in the sky. Dark purple and turquoise fabrics were also used. The growth from SEA AND SKY (Plate 11-7) to SEA AND SKY TRIAD (Plate 11-8) is more pronounced. When the first one was done, I thought triangles would be more appropriate. The light on the sea forms triangle shapes. I hoped using them would add a third level to the meaning.

At the same time I thought of the idea for THE NEXT FRONTIERS II (Plate 11-1, page 125), I also wanted to do a SUNSET SEA quilt (Plate 11-12). Several years later I did, but I had also done several underwater quilts developing my painting. You can see how the work progressed with several small quilts and the first SUNSET SEA. Earlier in the book, is my latest SUNSET SEA II (Plate 9-2, page 109). All the underwater quilts build on each other, with the latest one having the richest surface.

Trying the barest glimmer of an idea is the beginning. While working on that idea you will

PLATE 11-7. *SEA AND SKY, 43" x 55", Vicki L. Johnson, Soquel, California, © 1987. Photo by George R. Young. This is a return to the series started with DAY/NITE (Plate 1-8, page 21) where I put two elements together to suggest a third.*

probably have more. They will start to come to you faster than you can make the quilts. Keep track of your ideas in a sketchbook so you do not forget them. Then you can select the most promising from a wealth of ideas for the next quilt. But, ideas leave as quickly as they come so you must record them somehow.

CONCLUDING THOUGHTS

Let your right brain choose while you are working. Sometimes it is just a feeling that some-thing is right if you do not think too much and just flow with your ideas. Analyzing everything can kill your creativity. Trust your instincts. When I buy fabric, I do sometimes buy just because I know it will make great kelp or roofs, but I also buy fabric just because I like it. Often that fabric is the one of which I wish I had bought ten yards.

In my next quilt it is just what I need. Friends sometimes give me fabrics that I think at the time I will never use. Then they prove to be perfect for my next quilt. Things come your way that will work

PLATE 11-8. *SEA AND SKY TRIAD, 32" x 43", Vicki L. Johnson, Soquel, California, © 1988. Once SEA AND SKY was completed, I decided it would have worked better using triangles, so I did still another version. The triangles suggest the reflected light on the ocean which has triangular shapes.*

well if you let them. That is serendipity.

I am beginning to think creating art is not about capturing a moment, as we say the impressionists did, but about symbols and their meaning to us. Even with landscapes we are using things that have deeper layers of meaning for people. In my ROSE BARN (Plate 5-16, page 76), I used an existing building and this quilt can be appreciated simply as capturing a beautiful scene. But, roses and barns have many symbolic meanings.

To most, a rose is a symbol of femininity and growth. Barns are also rich as metaphors. Carl Jung says buildings represent our minds and walking through a house is wandering through our thoughts. A building covered with roses could be a metaphor for blossoming female creativity. Since I rather like this meaning and it is my work, that is how I choose to see this quilt. But, if you respond to the image, you bring your own thoughts to it and you may find some other layer of meaning. An artwork with many explanations has more importance to more people. It is only through the symbolic meanings that these many interpretations happen.

The paintings people choose for their walls

PLATE 11-9. *KELP VII, 24" x 23", Vicki L. Johnson, Soquel, California, © 1991. An early underwater quilt, this one has only sponging in the ocean and the colors are lighter.*

should give them a gut reaction, not simply be in the colors they chose for decoration. In my experience, if you select them for their gut reaction, you will learn much about yourself, which is infinitely more valuable than color coordinated decorating. In the end, the works will go together since you selected them, and will work with your rooms making them very personal. To me it is rather like a scrap quilt, the different colors make a totality beyond the stiff "three fabrics only" type of quilt.

As they say in *Star Wars*, "Use the Force." Relax and loosen up; your quilts will be better. We are making quilts because we want to, so have fun with them. Do not let anyone's opinion change your mind about what you are sure you want to do. Once finished, your family and friends will be very impressed with an original painted quilt. You may see where you could improve, but do not let that keep you from being proud of the results. The work is never what you have in your mind. Use the knowledge of how you can improve to push you on to better quilts. Every one I make teaches me something, so I am challenged to continue.

PLATE 11-10 *A SEAL IN THE KELP, 26" x 26", Vicki L. Johnson, Soquel, California, © 1992. Using the same drawing as KELP VII, I did deeper blue painting with some spattering.*

PLATE 11-11. *A SEAL WITH GARIBALDIS, 25" x 36", Vicki L. Johnson, Soquel, California, © 1994. In this recent underwater quilt, I spattered and flipped lots of color. Garibaldis add a bright contrast to the blue sea and repeat the amber tones in the kelp.*

PLATE 11-12. *SUNSET SEA, 60" x 84", Vicki L. Johnson, Soquel, California,*
© 1992. Photo by George R. Young. Sometimes I have several ideas at once and only
time to work on one quilt, which was true of this quilt and THE NEXT FRONTIERS
II. Recording the idea in a watercolor helped me remember until several years later
when I developed the sunset quilts.

Appendix

CONSTRUCTION OF A BASIC FOUR-PATCH

For those who are new to quilting, I am including directions for the method I use to sew squares together. If you have a method you are comfortable with, use it.

To keep my squares in place, I use pins in the corners to tell me where they belong while I am handling them for sewing. The top left corner square has a pin in its top left corner. Then I pin the second row to the top row (Plate A-1). These squares are then removed from the pinup board and

sewn. I leave the top left pin inserted so I do not turn the grouping. This group is then put back in place. You may find another method which helps you keep groupings in correct order.

For the example quilt I was using 3½" squares (allowing a ¼" seam allowance on each side), arranged in rows of four-patches with alternating solids and prints. Pick up a print and a solid and put them right sides together and run through the sewing machine with normal settings, but do not backstitch or cut the thread. Pick up the remaining two squares, put them right sides together and run them through the sewing machine. You could continue with more squares if you can keep track of your arrangement, chaining them together.

Cut the threads between the squares.

Press the seams both to the same side; do not iron the seam open. Ironing from the front will open the seam better without any pressed-in creases. Pin your patches on the pinup board with your painting after sewing so you know all are arranged correctly.

Still working in four-patch units, pick up two pairs and put them right sides together. Slide the two seams together and pin in the seam. Sew these together and again iron the seams from the top, but to one side. You should have a four-patch constructed. These are then sewn together into strips using the same technique of pinning.

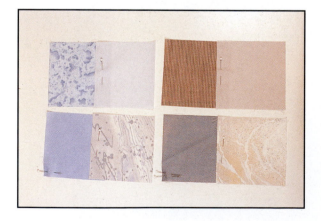

PLATE A-1.
When I remove patches from the pinup wall I put a pin in the upper left corner of each four-patch. With each pair pinned together, I know how to sew the four squares into a patch. The pin in the left corner helps me remember how to return the sewn patch to its position.

SOURCE LIST:

DHARMA TRADING CO.
P.O. Box 150916
San Rafael, CA 94915
(800) 542-5227 or
(415) 456-7657
Fax (415) 456-8747

Versatex,™ Createx™, other paint supplies and fabric. Excellent service.

COLOR CRAFT LTD.
14 Airport Park Rd. E
Granby, CT 06026
(800) 243-2712 or
(203) 653-5505
Fax (203) 653-0643

Createx™ paint. Manufacturer. Have pearlescent colors and covering white – minimum order $25.00 in 1995.

TESTFABRICS, INC.™
P. O. 420
Middlesex, NJ 08846
(908) 469-6446
Fax (908) 469-1147

Catalog and samples – $7.00. Cotton lawn 429w.

EXOTIC SILKS
252 State Street
Los Altos, CA 94022
(415) 948-8611

Silk reasonable, direct importer.

KEEPSAKE QUILTING
Route 25B, P.O. Box 1618
Centre Harbor, NH 03226-1618
(603) 253-8731
Fax (603) 253-8346

Fabric erasers, chalk wheels, marking pencils.

TREADLE ART
25834-I Narbonne Ave.
Lomita, CA 90717
(310) 534-5122
Orders (800) 327-4222
Fax (310) 534-8372

Presser feet for appliqué (open-toe) and spring needles. Also other tools.

WEB OF THREAD
3240 Lone Oak Road, Suite 124
Paducah, KY 42003
(800) 955-8185
(502) 554-8185
Fax (502) 554-8257

Many different threads.

THE ARTIST'S CLUB
5750 N.E. Hassalo
Portland, OR 97213
(800) 845-6507
Fax (503) 287-6916

Spatter brush and other brushes.

BINDERS
P.O. Box 53097
Atlanta, GA 30355
(800) 877-3242
Fax (404) 872-0294

Everything you need in artists' materials and Createx™ paints.

DANIEL SMITH INC.
4150 First Avenue South
P.O. Box 84268
Seattle, WA 98124-5568
(800) 426-6740
Fax (800) 238-4065

Artists' supplies at very good prices.

DICK BLICK
(800) 447-8192 orders

Artists' supplies, printing blocks 9" x 12" x ⅜".

INKO SCREEN PROCESS SUPPLIES
530 MacDonald Ave.
Richmond, CA 94801
(800) 955-8185 or (510) 235-8330
Fax (510) 235-1038

Everything you need to silkscreen and a book, too.

NASCO
(800) 558-9595
Fax (209) 545-1669 or (414) 563-8296

Sheet of rubber for stamps, 18" x 26".

PELLE'S
P.O. Box 242
Davenport, CA 95017
(408) 425-4743 phone/Fax

Rubber stamps & pads, marking pens: 4 sets of 6, press sheet.

THE PEDDLER'S WAGON
P.O. Box 109
Lamar, MO 64759-0109
(417) 682-3734

Preowned books – specializing in quilting books.

V & T GRAPHICS
225 Muir Dr.
Soquel, CA 95073
(408) 476-7567 phone/Fax

Vicki's quilts, notecards, paint, press sheets, spring needles.

Bibliography

PAINTING BOOKS

Blockley John. *Country Landscapes in Watercolor*. New York, NY: Watson-Guptill, 1989.

Good inspiration, but the work shown is on paper. John Blockley has several books. All that I have seen are good.

_____. *Getting Started in Watercolor*. Cincinnati, OH: North Light Books, 1985.

_____. *Watercolor Interpretations*. Cincinnati, OH: North Light Books, 1987.

Jerstorp, Karin and Eva Kohlmark. *The Textile Design Book*. Asheville, NC: Lark Books, 1988.

Excellent source of design ideas for use with paint. Emphasis with paint is on making fabric. Has good section on printing.

Kanzinger, Linda S. *The Complete Book of Fabric Painting*. Spokane, WA: The Alcott Press, 1986.

This is so complete it is best used as an encyclopedia. It is self-published, address below, $19.95 + $2 shipping. Also available through Dharma. The Alcott Press, P.O. Box 857, Spokane, WA 99210, (509) 326-3373.

Tate, Elizabeth. *The North Light Illustrated Book of Painting Techniques*. Cincinnati, OH: North Light Books, 1988.

Very interesting and complete book of painting techniques done with different media on surfaces other than fabric. Good ideas to try on fabric.

BOOKS ON PRINTING METHODS

Auvil, Kenneth. *Serigraphy, Silk Screen Techniques for the Artist*. NJ: Prentice-Hall, Inc., 1965.

In-depth coverage of the silk screen.

Inko Silk Screen Printing, Materials & Techniques. Richmond, CA: Inko Screen Process Co.

A guide to the silkscreen process written by a company that sells all the products discussed.

Johnston and Kaufman. *Design on Fabrics*. New York: Reinhold Pub., 1967.

Has good chapters on block printing and silkscreening, but uses dyes.

Proctor and Lew. *Surface Design for Fabric*. Seattle, WA: University of Washington Press, 1984.

Good coverage of stenciling including silkscreen and block printing. Does mention Versatex™, but most information is on dyes.

MACHINE STITCHING BOOKS

Bennett, D. J. *Machine Embroidery With Style*. Seattle, WA: Madrona Pub., 1980.

Fanning, Robbie. *The Complete Book of Machine Quilting*. Radnor, PA: Chilton Book Co., 1980.

Hargrave, Harriet. *Heirloom Machine Quilting. Revised*, Lafayette, CA: C & T Publishing, 1990.

Laury, Jean Ray. *Quilted Clothing*. Birmingham, AL: Oxmoor House, Inc., 1982.

Roberts, Sharee Dawn. *Creative Machine Art*. Paducah, KY: American Quilter's Society, 1992.

BOOKS FOR INSPIRATION

Cameron, Julia. *The Artist's Way*. New York: G.P. Putman's Sons, 1992.

Edwards, Betty. *Drawing on the Artist Within*. New York: Simon and Schuster, 1986.

For anyone wishing more information on creativity and ways to release it.

Jung, Carl G. *Man and His Symbols*. New York: Doubleday, 1964.

McMorris, Penny and Kile, Michael. *The Art Quilt*. San Francisco, CA: The Quilt Digest Press, 1986.

Segawa, Setsuko. *New Wave Quilt Collections*. Kyoto, Japan: Mitsumura Suiko Shoin Pub. Co., Ltd., 1991.

_____. *New Wave Quilt Collections II*. Kyoto, Japan: Mitsumura Suiko Shoin Pub. Co., Ltd., 1992.

Swim, Laurie. *Quilting*. New York, NY: Mallard Press, 1991.

CARE BOOKS AND PAMPHLETS

Gunn, Virginia. *Guide #3, The Care and Conservation of Quilts*. San Francisco, CA: American Quilt Study Group.

Korwin, Laurence. *Textiles as Art – Selecting, Framing, Mounting, Lighting and Maintaining Textile Art*. Chicago, IL, 1990.

Protecting Your Quilts, an Owner's Guide to Insurance, Care and Restoration, and Appraisal. Edited by Jeannie M. Spears. Appraisal Certification Committee, 1990, Paducah, KY: American Quilter's Society.

MAGAZINES AND CATALOGS

Aardvark Adventures, P.O. Box 2449, Livermore, CA 94550. (800) 388-ANTS (510) 443-ANTS.

Art/Quilt Magazine, 9543 Meadowbriar, Houston, TX 77063-3812.

Professional Quilter, Oliver Press, 104 Bramblewood Lane, Lewisberry, PA 17339-9535.

TreadleArt®, 25834-I Narbonne Ave., Lomita, CA 90717.

MAGAZINE ARTICLES

Quilter's Newsletter, April 1992, "The Right Stuff," Caroline Reardon, pp. 38–41.

Quilter's Newsletter, May 1993, No. 252, "Machine Quilting Tips Using the Darning Foot," Barbara Smith, pp. 29, 30.

Quilter's Newsletter, Sept. 1993, "Thread Wise," Robbie Fanning, pp. 48–49.

PREOWNED BOOKS

The Peddler's Wagon, P.O. Box 109, Lamar, MO 64759-0109, (417) 682-3734.

COPYRIGHT OFFICE:

Register of Copyright, Copyright Office, Library of Congress, Washington, DC 20559.

Quilt Index

American Quilter's Society
dedicated to publishing books for today's quilters

These books can be found in local bookstores and quilt shops. If you are unable to locate a title in your area, you can order by mail from AQS, P.O. Box 3290, Paducah, KY 42002-3290. Please add $2 for the first book and 40¢ for each additional one to cover postage and handling. (International orders please add $2.50 for the first book and $1 for each additional one.)